ROUTLEDGE LIBRARY EDITIONS:
JAPAN

A STUDY OF SHINTO

A STUDY OF SHINTO
The Religion of the Japanese Nation

GENCHI KATO

Volume 82

Routledge
Taylor & Francis Group

LONDON AND NEW YORK

First published in English in 1926

This edition first published in 2011
by Routledge
2 Park Square, Milton Park, Abingdon, Oxon, OX14 4RN

Simultaneously published in the USA and Canada
by Routledge
270 Madison Avenue, New York, NY 10016

Routledge is an imprint of the Taylor & Francis Group, an informa business

© 1926, 1971 Genchi Kato

Printed and bound in Great Britain

British Library Cataloguing in Publication Data
A catalogue record for this book is available from the British Library

ISBN 13: 978-0-415-56498-4 (Set)
eISBN 13: 978-0-203-84317-8 (Set)
ISBN 13: 978-0-415-59349-6 (Volume 82)
eISBN 13: 978-0-203-84215-7 (Volume 82)

Publisher's Note
The publisher has gone to great lengths to ensure the quality of this reprint but
points out that some imperfections in the original copies may be apparent.

Disclaimer
The publisher has made every effort to trace copyright holders and would
welcome correspondence from those they have been unable to trace.

GENCHI KATO

A STUDY OF SHINTO

The Religion of the Japanese Nation

CURZON PRESS

First published in Tokyo 1926

Second edition 1971

Curzon Press Ltd · London and Dublin

SBN 7007 0007 2

Printed in Hungary

PREFACE

This work was first published over four decades ago by Professor Kato as a contribution to the international understanding of Japanese religious attitudes. The validity of his argument in the meantime has by no means been diminished whilst the obligation laid upon the occidental world to understand and even to appreciate this form of religious concept, its genesis, development and undoubtedly too its relevance to contemporary circumstances, remains compulsive.

Hitherto, the author has argued, most Western students of things Japanese have viewed Shinto, and made public their impressions of it, only as a rather primitive nature religion, and its ethico-intellectualistic aspect in a later and more highly developed form is seldom set forth with adequate thoroughness. To such students Shinto may seem even now, like the religion of ancient Egypt or that of Babylonia, to be of mere archaic interest, with no bearing on the actual life of the Japanese of today. Thus, for example, in Aston's larger book, *Shinto, the Way of the Gods*, the naturalistic aspect of the religion has been dealt with in detail but, to a great extent, its development in the field of ethics and the human intellect is left almost unexplored.

Nevertheless, he continues, Shinto is by no means to be classed with the religions of the past. It is alive; moreover it is very vitally active in the ethico-religious consciousness and national life of the patriotic Japanese of today. Shinto is, and therefore should be so regarded, like Christianity, Buddhism or Islam, one of the world's living religions. It has passed through a lengthy meandering course of development parallel with the national life of Japan. Starting as a form of nature worship, it has evolved itself into a peculiar form of religion in which ethics and the intellect are intimately related. While intrinsically national in itself it has, at different times, assimilated spiritualistic nourishment in the form of Confucian ethics and Buddhistic philosophy so that today it stands stronger perhaps than ever before, inseparably interwoven in the national life of the Japanese race.

The chief purpose of this treatise is thus to investigate and present, so far as it may briefly do, the salient features of Shinto through a long history of development from its remote past up to the present, through its lower stages up to that of today, the method employed being not in the least dogmatic but strictly historical throughout. In other words, it endeavours to make a genetical or historical study of Shinto from a scientific point of view, desiring thereby to illustrate the higher aspects of the religion to a degree hitherto left unattempted by the occidental students of the Orient, and at the same time, perhaps, to offer to other investigators a convenient text-book, altogether free from preconceptions, compiled on strict lines of religious comparison.

This work may therefore be regarded as a pioneer effort to present, by the light of modern research in the comparative science of religion, the salient features of the Shinto faith in its origin, growth and development, and thus provides an important contribution to Western understanding of the Japanese mind.

London, 1970.

Publishers' Note

In this reprint of the main text
the original spelling Shintō has
been retained throughout.

CONTENTS

ABBREVIATIONS USED

A. K. y.   *Azumakagami*, edited by Yoshikawa-Hanshichi
吾妻鏡 (吉川半七本）

B. Z.   *Bukkyō-Zensho* 佛敎全書

E. T. K.   B. H. Chamberlain, English Translation of the *Kojiki*

E. T. Kg.   G. Katō and H. Hoshino, English Translation of the *Kogoshūi* (2nd edition)

E. T. N.   W. G. Aston, English Translation of the *Nihongi*

G. R. k.   *Gunsho-Ruijū* (Keizai-Zasshisha edition)
群書類從 (經濟雜誌社本）

H. Z.   *Hyakka-Zeirin* 百家說林

J. Z.   *Jingi-Zensho* 神祇全書

K. T.   *Kokushi-Taikei* 國史大系

N. B. Z. h.   *Nihon-Bungaku-Zensho* (Hakubunkan edition)
日本文學全書 (博文館本）

N. D.   *Nihon-Daizōkyō* 日本大藏經

S. S.   *Shintō-Sōsho* 神道叢書

S. T.   *Shintō-Sōsetsu* 神道叢說

T. A. S. J.   *Transactions of the Asiatic Society of Japan*

Z. G. R. k.   *Zoku-Gunsho-Ruijū* (Keizai-Zasshisha edition)
續群書類從 (經濟雜誌社本）

Z. Z. G. R. k.   *Zoku-Zoku-Gunsho-Ruijū* (Kokusho-Kankōkai edition)
續々群書類從 (國書刊行會本）

A STUDY OF SHINTO, THE RELIGION
OF THE JAPANESE NATION

BOOK I INTRODUCTION

I

Two Main Divisions of Shintō—The Sectarian Shintō and the State Shintō

There are thirteen Shintō sects now living and officially recognized as religions in Japan, on the same footing as Buddhism and Christianity. These sects are (1) the Fusōkyō, (2) the Jikkōkyō, (3) the Kurozumikyō, (4) the Misogikyō, (5) the Tenrikyō, (6) the Konkōkyō, (7) the Shinrikyō, (8) the Taiseikyō, (9) the Shinshūkyō, (10) the Ontakekyō, (11) the Shūseiha, (12) the Shintōhonkyoku, and (13) the Taishakyō. Those numbered from (1) to (6) and, to a certain extent, also number (7), existed as religious Shintō sects in the Tokugawa Regime (1600—1867), while the six numbered (8) to (13) came into existence as independent Shintō sects in the Meiji Era (1868—1912), although some of both groups may be said to have a far remoter origin in ancient times or even in the Divine Age. State

Shintō, termed by certain foreign scholars patriotic
Shintō, is subdivided by some Japanese scholars into
two parts: one is called Jinsha (Jinja) Shintō, which
is concretely represented in the Shintō rites performed
by Shinkan and Shinshoku or Shintō priests who are
all secular government officials *in jure* in Jinsha (Jinja)
or Shintō shrines—buildings in the plain, simple style
of old—dedicated to Kami or Shintō deities, while the
other called Kokutai Shintō consists of ethical teachings
or moral instructions inseparably connected with the
unique national organization and history of the Japanese
people, formulated in the " Edict on Education " issued
by the late Emperor Meiji in the year 1890 (about
the middle of the Meiji Era), and now inculcated in
schools throughout the Empire.

So far as State Shintō is concerned, it may be taken
as a kind of national ceremony and teaching of Japanese
morality, and to that extent it might be called secular,
and non-religious, but, as investigation proceeds, the
truth will appear that even this State Shintō, which
some Japanese go so far as to speak of as no religion at
all, is in reality nothing short of evidence of a religion
interwoven in the very texture of the original beliefs
and national organization of the people, camouflaged
though it may be as a mere code of national ethics and
State rituals, and as such apparently entitled only to
secular respect.

The present writer, as his readers will soon be informed, advances the view that Shintō—the State Shintō as well as the Sectarian Shintō—is in very truth a religion, *i. e.,* the original religion of the Japanese people, or, otherwise stated, the religion of the Japanese people from the very beginning down to the present time.

II

WHAT IS MEANT BY RELIGION

What is meant by religion? In response to this question, an ordinary Christian will answer by giving to the term "religion" the sense or signification of Christianity, while a Buddhist will reply from the standpoint of his own faith. So, likewise, the Romantic Christian theologian Schleiermacher stands diametrically opposed to Hegel, the philosopher of panlogism,—the former thinking that religion is in essence "the feeling of absolute dependence", while the latter finds its essence in "freedom" *i. e.,* independence. Since dependence and independence or freedom are two conditions incompatible with each other, it may seem that there is no definition of religion among scholars agreed upon at all. And yet, thanks to recent development of the science of religion, the student of that science has arrived at a golden mean of definition, which is neither too Buddhistic nor too Christian, taking into consideration each and every religion, from its lowest stage to the highest. As a student of the science of religion, after long and pains-taking study, I wish to define religion as *One's consciousness of being in a special relationship with the Divine.* Here by "the Divine" I mean any religious object or objects, be they Christian or be they Buddhistic or be they of any other religious creed, whether in a lower order of religion or in a higher order of religion in the course of development—the Almighty God of the Christians or the omniscient Buddha as the God of gods (Skt. Devatīdeva), an ancestral deity or a fetish-god, disembodied spirits or divine totemic animals, a god (gods) in theocratic (deocentric) religion or a god (gods) in theanthropic (homocentric) religion. If a man comes into relation with such an object (or objects) of religion, which is greater and stronger than man himself, and so far mysterious, unfathomable, incomprehensible, transcending the limit of human knowledge, at least at some moment of time, therefore superior to man in some sense or other, if a religious object (or objects) so understood is put into relation with a man, just as a son is related with his father, and a friend with a friend, or if a man has faith in such a kind of religious object (or objects) and he believes that, for instance, his prayers are granted, then we meet a fact or phenomenon, which can be characteristically termed "religious".

From what I have just explained, the definition of

religion which I have given above may be re-stated in a somewhat different way, though in the same spirit, as follows:— Religion is a man's humanly entering into relation with Something superhuman or what transcends man. Or, Religion is a practical mood of a man's mind towards the Divine. Or, Religion is a practical establishment of a man's vital relationship with Something superhuman or what transcends man. Or, Religion is a man's vital experience (*Erlebnis* in German) of his being with the Divine or his being entirely united with the Divine (complete union of a man with the Divine).

In concluding this section I may add that the expression, a man's "being in a special relationship with the Divine", which proves to be the essence of religion, embraces two different aspects, while it shows, though differently, only one and the same essence of religion. These two aspects of religion may be termed theocratic (or deocentric) and theanthropic (or homocentric). In the field of theocratic religion, a man's "being in a special relationship with the Divine" may be characterized as a man's life *with* the Divine, or, Divine communion of a man, while in the theanthropic or homocentric branch of religion, a man's being in a special relation with the Divine may mean a man's complete union or oneness with the Divine, here we find the complete union of divinity and humanity, or, in other words, we see divinity manifesting itself in humanity, *i. e.*, *Deus-Homo*, technically speaking. In either case, it can be easily seen that religion is neither more nor less than what is implied in my definition of religion mentioned above, which interprets religion as "A man's vital experience of his being with the Divine or his being entirely united with the Divine or complete union of a man with the Divine". Needless to say, this definition of religion comprehends all religions, high or low, natural or ethico-intellectualistic, theocratic or theanthropic, national (tribal) or universal, propagandistic (proselytising) or non-propagandistic (non-proselytising).

BOOK II GENETICAL OR HISTORICAL

PART I SHINTŌ IN THE STAGE OF NATURE RELIGION

SECTION I PRE-POLYDEMONISTIC AND POLYDEMONISTIC STAGES OF SHINTŌ

CHAPTER I

SOME TRACES OF ANIMATISM OR PRE-ANIMISM IN SHINTŌ

We often see a phase of religion among nature peoples which tells us that in that stage of religious development the object of their worship is one that directly appeals to our senses: for instance, they worship the sun, *i. e.*, not the spirit of the sun, but the sun itself, visible to the naked eye; they worship the wind, *i. e.*, the wind palpable to our senses, and not the invisible mysterious power residing in the wind. Thus also the visible Heaven itself, the high awe-inspiring mountain itself, the roaring sea itself, the tremendous cataract itself, and so on, are all worshipped as divine. This is what we call simple or original nature worship or animatism, or pre-polydemonism in general, in contradistinction to animism or polydemonism, because in the stage of animism or polydemonism people believe in spiritual powers, either incorporated or disembodied, *i. e.,* the crude philosophy of animism or polydemonism presupposes the existence of a spirit or invisible divine power inherent in the visible object of Nature ; they worship the former by and through the latter, and not the latter itself.   In ancient Egypt, for instance, the Sun-Gods Ra and Aten in origin were in the stage of pre-animism or animatism, and by degrees they passed on to the stage of animism; in Babylonia, the Sun-God Shamash has the same history ; this is the case with Zeus, the Heavenly God of ancient Greece, and the Greek Hermes, originally an upright stone itself on the boundary, as the very name of the God shows.   In Vedic India the Wind-God Vātā represents a wind-god in the stage of animatism, while Vāyū, God of the wind, is produced in the animistic stage of Indian religion.   The case is the same with the deities of Shintō.   We can discover a trace or remnant of simple nature worship once existing in Shintō, the most primitive form of religious belief among the Japanese.   In the *Hishi-zume-no-Matsuri-no-Norito* or *Ritual of the Festival of Appeasing the Fire-God,* the physically visible fire and the God residing in the fire are indiscriminately and interchangeably referred to, there having been no distinction at all between the God of Fire and the physical fire itself, visible to our naked eyes. The history of the development of the Vedic Fire-God Agni tells the same thing. In ancient Japan the God of Fire was called Kagutsuchi, the Radiant (Shining) One, or Homusubi, the Fire-Producer, and there was little or no distinction between the God of Fire and the physical fire itself. So we read in the *Hishizume-no-Matsuri-no-Norito* or *Ritual of the Festival of Appeasing the Fire-God*:—

"When Izanami's last son Homusubi, *God of Fire*, was born, her pudenda were burnt and she passed away......And lo! giving birth to *Fire*, her pudenda were burnt."

Here we see the words fire and the God of Fire indiscriminately used by the same author, meaning one and the same thing. On this point I agree with Aston's view.[1] The ancient Japanese seem to have had the same belief as regards the wind, namely, I think they may have made very little distinction between the god in the wind (like the Indian Vāyū) and the palpable wind (like the Indian Vāta) itself. On reference to the Japanese historical books, *e. g.*, the *Nihongi* or *Chronicles of Japan* and the *Kujiki* or *Chronicles of the Old Matters of Former Ages*, we find that the Japanese mind at that time made little distinction or none at all between the God of the Wind and the wind itself.

[1] W. G. Aston, *Shintō the Way of the Gods*, p. 316.

In the *Nihongi* we have a passage which describes how the corpse of a traitor, Amewakahiko by name, was brought back from the earth up to the Plain of High Heaven, and on that occasion the name of the messenger sent from Heaven for the purpose is differently mentioned, in one account as Hayachi-no-kami or God of the Wind and in another as the physical wind itself. And it seems to me that, to the ancient Japanese, the sun, the moon, seas, rivers, mountains, trees and herbs, and the Great-Eight-Island-Country, *i. e.*, the Land of Japan, itself, are all living beings, offspring of the divine male Izanagi and the divine female Izanami, and so far those natural objects are regarded as in reality supernatural or mysterious superhuman beings, *i. e.*, Kami[1] (Deities).

On this point the present writer completely agrees with the learned Moto-ori that there was in ancient Japan a simple nature worship in the adoration of the sun, the moon, seas, mountains, rivers,....and trees (*Vide* Moto-ori-Norinaga, *Kojikiden* or *Commentary on the Kojiki*, Vol. VI. *Collected Works*, Vol. I, pp. 151, 357. *Ise-Futamiya-Sakitake-no-Ben. Collected Works*, Vol. IV, p. 739).

Therefore we read in the *Manyōshū* or *Collection of a Myriad Leaves* :—

[1] Thus we have the expression " Shintō " or " Kami-no-Michi," " The Way of the Deities or Gods " (or " The Divine Way ").

"The highest peak of Mt. Fuji[1] ....is a wondrous deity.......and a guardian of the land of Japan........" (*Manyōshū*, Vol. III).

So we are told that there was in the beginning no shrine dedicated to any deity on Mt. Fuji, it is because the mountain itself is a divinity. The famous Mt. Tsukuba in Hitachi Province is also itself a divinity, so in the *Manyōshū* (*ibid*.), the male and female peaks are styled the "Mated Deities standing side by side."

According to the *Nihongi*, in the year 692 in the reign of the Empress Jitō, Imperial messengers were sent to the celebrated mountains and rivers of the land to pray to them for rain (*E. T. N.*, Vol II, pp. 407, 408). In this case, it seems to me that the mountains and rivers are themselves deities.

Even as late as the 14th century, it seems to me that according to Saka-Shibutsu's *Daijingū-Sankeiki* or *Diary of My Pilgrimage to the Ise Shrine* there still existed in Ise a simple nature worship in the form of dendrolatry, deifying and worshipping a cherry tree called "Sakura-no-Miya" in the precincts of the Grand Ise Shrine.

Thunder itself, to the simple mind of the ancient

---

[1] "But a wondrous deity it surely is!
   Of Yamato, the Land of Sunrise,
      It is the peace-giver, it is the God, it is the treasure"
            (Aston, *History of Japanese Literature*, pp. 40, 41).

Japanese, is also nothing but a Narukami or Thundering
Deity, in other words, they made a simple nature
worship of the thunder peals. The *Honchō-Seiki*, an
historical book of the Japanese, describes Thunder as a
comet-like apparition, which comes flying down to
house roofs and destroys[1] them.

---

[1] This we find in a description of the year 1146 in the reign of the
Emperor Konoe. *Vide K. T.*, Vol. VIII, p. 525.

Compare the animatisms of the Chinese, the Greeks, and the Romans
(W. Hopkins, *History of Religions*, pp. 240, 494. Clifford Moore, *Religious
Thought of the Greeks*, p. 225).

CHAPTER II

ANIMISTIC PHASES OF NATURE WORSHIP AMONG THE JAPANESE—COMPLEX NATURE WORSHIP

As we have already seen, on one hand, the sun itself was divine, the visible sun-disc or solar orb was a divinity; on the other, the sun was completely humanized, endowed with human passions and will, acting as a sentient being, endowed with male or female sex. So we see that the Deity of the Sun is Amaterasu-Ōmikami or the Heaven-Shining-Great-August-Deity, otherwise called Ōhirumemuchi-no-Kami or the Female Possessor of the Great Sun, *i. e.*, the Spirit of the Sun, who had quarrels with her impetuous brother Susano-o-no-Mikoto and at last took refuge in the Heavenly Rock-Cave.

Moreover, the ancient Japanese had a morning sun-goddess, called Wakahirume-no-Mikoto, interpreted, by a later commentator, as a younger sister of Amaterasu-Ōmikami, who was herself the great midday sun. Hiruko is a sun-god, in contradistinction to the great Sun-Goddess Amaterasu-Ōmikami and her divine sister Wakahirume-no-Mikoto. Misguided by the Chinese characters, even the learned Moto-ori-Norinaga literally interpreted Hiruko as a "leech child," while the celebrated novelist Bakin, Shikida-Toshiharu and Prof. K. A. Florenz understood by Hiruko a child born of the sun, in other words, a small or young sun, *i. e.*, a star.[1]

It may be remarked, in passing, that in Japan the Sun-God Hiruko early gave place to the Sun-Goddess[2] Ōhirumemuchi-no-Kami, as similarly in Argos the female Heaven Dione[3], the counterpart of Zeus, the male Heaven, was long forgotten, while Zeus alone enjoyed supreme divine power, and in Homer was revered as the father and king of gods and men.

These are nature deities personified in one respect in a garb of Japanese mythology and may be considered products of the religious consciousness of complex nature worship among the ancient Japanese.

Tsukuyomi-no-Mikoto, or Tsukuyomi-Otoko, the male moon walking along the nightly sky, as one of the poets of the *Manyōshū* put it, is also a god produced in the stage of the religious consciousness characterized as complex nature worship.

The stars never occupied any significant position in original Shintō belief, though there are aspects of the evil god—Amatsu-Mikahoshi, the August Star of Heaven, otherwise Amatsu-Kagaseo, the Brilliant Male.

---

1 *Vide* Bakin, *Gendō-Hōgen. H. Z.*, Vol. Ia, p. 439. K. A. Florenz, *Orientalische Religionen*, S. 198 (*Kultur der Gegenwart*).

2 *Shikida-Toshiharu, Kojiki-Hyōchū,* Vol. Ia.

3 *Cf.* E. O. Barton, *Religions of the World*, p. 247.
  And also *vide* G. Murray, *Five Stages of Greek Religion*, p. 77.

Later on, greatly influenced by both Chinese and Buddhistic beliefs, the Japanese Star-God was identified with the Polar Star Myōken (Skt. Sudarśana), and finally through it with Ame-no-Minakanushi-no-Kami, the Divine Lord of the Very Centre of Heaven—the Supreme Deity of Heaven.

In the animistic stage of religious development in which trees and herbs were endowed with the power of speech, Thunder was a "God on high"[1] (Takatsu-Kami).

Susano-o-no-Mikoto was, mythologically speaking, a God of the Rainstorm while Kuraokami or Takaokami is a God of Rain; and the primitive Wind-God was differentiated into two, *viz.*, Ame-no-Mihashira or the Heavenly August Pillar, and Kuni-no-Mihashira or the Earthly August Pillar, in one of the Shintō Rituals[2]; and the Wind-God was sexually differentiated, as Shinatsuhiko or God of the Wind and Shinatsuhime or Goddess of the Wind, in the *Kojiki*.

Ōwatatsumi-no-Kami, the God or Spirit of the Sea, is the Japanese Poseidon; Ōyamatsumi-no-Kami is the God or Spirit of the Mountain. As early as the reign of Keikō-Tennō, the Emperor, observing the sublime beauty of high mountain ranges in a certain district

1 *Vide* K. A. Florenz, *Ōharai-no-Norito* or *Ritual of the Great Purification* (*T. A. S. J.*), p. 61 and note 47.

2 Sir E. Satow, *Ancient Japanese Rituals* (*T. A. S. J.*), Part II, pp. 436, 437.

of Kyūshū, asked if there dwelt a deity in the mountains, and one of his followers answered that there was a goddess called Yametsuhime in the mountains—a remarkable feminine counterpart of the so-called Yamabiko or Male of the mountains, literally translated.

Here we see clearly the distinction made by the ancient Japanese religious consciousness between the Deity of the mountain and the visible mountain itself. The case is the same with the relation between the celebrated Chinese mountain T'ai Shan and its God or Guardian Spirit called T'ai Shan Fu Chün.

According to the *Kogoshūi* or *Gleanings from Ancient Stories* written by Imbe-no-Hironari in 807, we have the Guardian Spirits of the Imperial court-grounds called "Ikasuri" and the Guardian Spirits of the Ōyashima or Great-Eight-Island-Country called "Ikushima" (*E. T. Kg.*, pp. 34, 35 and notes 62, 66).

In the period of the Empress Regnant Suiko (599), the Government Authorities ordered the people to worship the Deity of the Earthquake[1] (*E. T. N.*, Vol. II,

---

1 Aston mentions in a note to his English translation of the *Nihongi* that there were shrines in the Home Provinces dedicated to the Deity of the Earthquake in the reign of the Emperor Shōmu (701-756), but it seems to me that he has misread the Chinese characters of the *Shoku-Nihongi* passage 遣使畿內七道諸國檢看破地震神社 (Vol. XI. *K. T.*, Vol. II, p. 194), which means "The Government officials were ordered to proceed to the Home Provinces and the Seven Circuits to inspect those shrines damaged by the earthquake that occurred there." According to Aston, 破地震神社 means "the shrines dedicated to the Deity of the Earthquake that suffered damage," but the correct meaning of the passage in question is, in my opinion, "the shrines, sacred to some deities, which were damaged by the earthquake" (*Vide* Aston, *E. T. N.*, Vol. II, p. 124).

p. 124 and note 2).

According to the *Nihon-Sandai-Jitsuroku* (Vol. XLVIII. *K. T.*, Vol. IV, p. 671), a local governor purified himself and brought offerings to the Deity of Mt. Kaimon, an eruptive volcano in Satsuma Province, in order to appease divine anger.

It is recorded that in the reign of the Emperor Nimmyō (843) the Deity of the hot springs of Tama-tsukuri was accorded the Lower Grade of the Junior Fifth Court Rank (*Shoku-Nihonkōki*, Vol. XIII. *K. T.*, Vol. III, p. 343).

We find the Japanese Pluto in Yomotsu-Kami, or the Deity of the Underworld, with whom Izanami-no-Mikoto had a talk in her descent to the Yomi-no-Kuni or Dark Region, where she remained and afterwards herself became the Great Goddess of the Underworld. She occupies a position in Japanese mythology some-what similar to that held in Hindoo mythology by the Indian Yama, who was the first mortal that died.

We have a kind of Japanese dendrolatry in Kuku-nochi, the Master or Spirit of trees, and Kayanohime, the Mistress or Spirit of grass, and Toyoukehime-no-Kami, a cereal goddess, or the Spirit of the rice plant, mentioned in the *Nihongi* and the *Norito* of the *Engi-shiki* or *Institutes of the Engi Period*[1] (901–923). And

---

1 *Vide* W. G. Aston, *E. T. N.*, Vol. I, p. 18.

Vide also Sir E. Satow, English translation of the *Ōtonohogai-no-Norito* or *Ritual of Luck-Wishing of the Great Palace* (*T. A. S. J.*), p. 190.

popularly even nowadays we have the expression "kodama," *i. e.*, the spirit of a tree.

The Amatsu-Himorogi or Heavenly Sacred Trees are revered, because they are connected with some divine spirits represented by or embodied in them.

Examples of Japanese zoolatry or theriolatry are also numerous in the old documents : first of all the serpent was worshipped as divine, so that we find the Deity of Mt. Mimoro in the form of a great serpent, according to the *Nihongi* (*E. T. N.*, Vol. I, p. 347); and in the *Hitachifudoki* or *Ancient Topography of Hitachi Province*, compiled in the 6th year of Wadō (713) in the reign of the Empress Gemmyō, there are mentioned mountain deities that are nothing but the veritable serpents of the locality.[1]

Besides, we must remember that the deity whom Susano-o-no-Mikoto regarded as an awe-inspiring divinity was the great monster serpent, according to the *Nihongi*, that made its appearance and devoured a young maiden offered to it as a human sacrifice each year (*E. T. N.*, Vol. I, p. 56).

Moreover, the wolf is a deity, sometimes called "Ōkuchi-no-Kami" or "Deity with wide-open mouth" (Kurita, *Kofudoki-Itsubunkōshō*, Vol. I, p. 25).

The tiger is also a kami or a fearful deity (*E. T. N.*, Vol. II, p. 36), the hare and the white wild boar are

[1]   *Vide* Kurita, *Hyōchū-Kofudoki*, p. 15.

deities also, according to the *Kojiki* (*E. T. K.*, p. 217), and we read in the *Nihongi* the theophany of a certain mountain deity in the form of a white deer (*ibid.*, Vol. I, p. 208); even a silkworm or a louse is a deity[1] (*E. T. N.*, Vol. II, p. 188, and *Ōsumifudoki* or *Ancient Topography of Ōsumi Province. Cf.* Kurita, *Kofudoki-Itsubunkōshō*). The Yatagarasu or Eight-hand-span Crow, *i. e.*, Large Crow, is a deity and there is a shrine sacred to it in Uda-no-Kōri, Yamato Province (*E. T.N.*, Vol. I, pp. 115, 116. *Engishiki-Shimmyōchō. K. T.*, Vol. XIII, p. 292).

The famous golden kite which came flying to welcome the Emperor Jimmu while proceeding on an expedition to Yamato Province is also a divine bird having some connection with the Sun-Goddess, believed to be the Ancestress of the Japanese Imperial family (*E. T. N.*, Vol. I, p. 127). The crocodile is a great deity, according to the *Kojiki* (*E. T. K.*, p. 125), called "Sabimochi-no-Kami," the Deity-Blade-Possessor, and was worshipped by a certain Kuhao, according to the *Settsufudoki* or *Ancient Topography of Settsu Province* (Kurita, *Kofudoki-Itsubunkōshō*, Vol. I, p. 47).

Besides those animals that are themselves deities, we have several others that are regarded as divine

---

[1] Among the ancient Egyptians, we find the divine beetle *scarab*, and among the Bushmen the divine insect *ngo* (A. Menzies, *History of Religion*, first edition, p. 127. Alexander le Roy, *Religion of the Primitives*, p. 74).

messengers. For instance, the deer is a divine messenger from the Deity of Kasuga, the monkey from the Deity of Hie, the pigeon from the God Hachiman, the fox from the Inari Deity, the snowy heron from the Deity of Kehi, the tortoise from the Deity of Matsunō, the crow from the Deity of Kumano, etc. (*Shintō-Myōmoku-Ruijushō*, Vol. VI, p. 13).

CHAPTER III

FETISHISM AND PHALLICISM

Fetish objects abound in primitive Shintō. The "Ten Sacred Auspicious Treasures" are a heavenly heritage from Nigihayahi-no-Mikoto down to his son Umashimade-no-Mikoto, according to the *Kujiki*.[1] The "Ten Sacred Auspicious Treasures" comprise:— the Mirror of the Offing, the Mirror of the Shore, the Eight-hand-span Sword, the Life-inspiring Jewel, the Jewel of Perfect Health and Strength, the Jewel of Resuscitating the Dead, the Jewel Warding Evil from Roads, the Serpent-preventing Scarf, the Bee-preventing Scarf, and the Scarfs of Various Materials and Efficacies (*Cf. E. T. N.*, Vol. II, pp. 264, 321, 322, 373; Aston, *Shintō, the Way of the Gods*, p. 293. *Cf.* Chap. X).

These ten treasures are separated into four classes, namely, the mirrors, the sword, the jewels, and the scarfs. Omitting the last mentioned class there remain three, which constitute the Divine Imperial Regalia,[2] the Triple Divine Heirlooms of the Imperial

[1] Although the authorship of the *Kujiki* is uncertain and its genuineness is much disputed by native scholars, yet it is a very old book, and part of it is almost as authentic as the *Kojiki* and the *Nihongi*.

[2] These three consist of the Yata-no-Kagami or Eight-hand-span Mirror, the Kusanagi-no-Tsurugi or Herb-quelling Sword and the Yasakani-no-Magatama or Ever-bright Curved Jewels, and are the triple symbolical heirlooms of the legitimate Sovereign of Japan.

line—like the Pusaka of the natives of the East Indies, or the Churinga[1] of the Central Australians.

And, moreover, the *Kujiki* attributes some supernatural miraculous virtues to the mirrors, the sword, the jewels, and the scarfs, for the book says, "These Ten Sacred Auspicious Treasures, if shaken, will restore life to the dead and cure physical pain" (*Tennō-Hongi. K. T.*, Vol. VII, p. 322).

From the above it may readily be inferred that the Sanshu-no-Jingi or Three Divine Imperial Regalia, in common with the other items of the "Ten Sacred Auspicious Treasures," partook, in ancient times, somewhat of the nature of fetishes.

Miraculous virtues are attributed to the Murakumo[2] or Kusanagi Sword, extracted by Susano-o-no-Mikoto from the tail of the monster serpent in Izumo Province, with which the Imperial Prince Yamato-takeru-no-Mikoto mowed grass in the plain of Yaizu, Suruga Province, and thereby, thanks to the miraculous virtue of the divine sword, made a narrow escape from being burnt to death by the treacherous Ainu enemy (*E. T. N.*, Vol. I, p. 205).

The same Prince, notwithstanding his bravery and courage, was, however, fatally attacked by the evil

1 *Vide* Durkheim, *Elementary Forms of the Religious Life* (pp. 119–123).

2 Literally, "Murakumo Sword" means "Sword of Assembled Clouds." "Kusanagi Sword" means "Herb-quelling Sword."

mountain deity when he ascended Mt. Ibuki leaving the divine Kusanagi Sword behind at the house of his consort Miyasuhime, in Owari, and so being without its unseen supernatural protection.

We have a similar case of the belief in the miraculous virtue inherent in the sword in Japan, when we are informed through a graphical description of the sword in the *Heike-Monogatari* that the warrior Minamoto-no-Yoritomo, while young, was taken prisoner by his enemy Heike as soon as the divine influence of the Higekiri Sword, the inherited sacred treasure of his own House, had ceased to protect him, owing to his casual separation from it.[1]

Similarly in the reign of the Emperor Suinin we are told that a sword miraculously crossed the sea of its own accord to the Island of Awaji, where the devout islanders received it with reverence and built a shrine to it, according to the *Nihongi* narration (*E. T. N.*, Vol. I, p. 186).

Since the eastern expedition of Prince Yamato-takeru as early as the reign of the Emperor Keikō, the Kusanagi Sword, one of the Three Divine Imperial Regalia, has been enshrined at Atsuta, in Owari Province, as a deity under the charge of Shintō priests there—the present Great Government Shrine of Atsuta (*E. T. N.*, Vol. I, p. 56).

1   *Vide N. B. Z. h.* ("*On the Sword*").

So, in the reign of the Emperor Tenchi (623–668),
when Dōgyō, a Buddhist priest of Shiragi (Silla),
attempted in vain to steal the divine Kusanagi Sword,
preserved in the Holy of Holies at Atsuta, intending
to make off with it to his native Korea, the miraculous
virtue of the Sword prevented the would-be thief from
accomplishing his sacrilegious purpose (*E. T. N.*, Vol.
II, p. 290. *E. T. Kg.*, pp. 46, 85. *Cf.* Hayashi-Razan,
Honchō-Jinjakō or *Studies on the Japanese Shintō
Shrines*, Vol. III, p. 29).

A curse by the Kusanagi Sword brought disease
to the Emperor Temmu in 686, so diviners declared,
and the Emperor was thereupon constrained to return
the Sword to its shrine at Atsuta in Owari, whence
it had been removed.

The case is the same with the Yata-no-Kagami
or Divine Mirror, one of the Three Divine Imperial
Regalia. In the reign of the Emperor Yūryaku, the
Divine Mirror of the Ise Shrine, according to the
tradition of the *Nihongi*, was concealed in the ground
at a certain spot on the banks of the sacred Isuzu
River by the Imperial Guardian Priestess of the
Mirror, Princess Takuhata by name, at her suicidal
death, when a miraculous rainbow made its appearance,
indicating, as it were, the very spot where the Mirror
was buried (*E. T. N.*, Vol. I, p. 341).

In later times on every occasion that the Imperial

Palace in Kyôto was destroyed by fire, as repeatedly
happened, the Mirror more or less prominently displayed its miraculous virtue and proved itself divine.
With these manifestations in mind Imbe-no-Hironari
mentions in his book *Kogoshūi* that the Sword and
the Mirror were assuredly charms or talismans of the
August Person of the Emperor (*E. T. Kg.*, pp. 35, 37,
72, 73).

The miraculous power of the Divine Sword and
Mirror against an enemy reminds us of that wondrous
virtue attributed to Yahweh's Ark from whose presence on the battlefield the bitterest foes of Israel
shrank, as related in the *Old Testament*. Tradition
ascribes similar miraculous virtue to the Divine
Mirror.

To cite a remarkable instance well illustrating
this point : According to the historical book *Azumakagami*, at the sanguinary naval battle of Dannoura
in the Inland Sea between the Genji and the Heike
some soldiers of the former fought their way to one
of the warships of the latter and were so audacious
as to make a blasphemous attempt to unlock the lid
of the sacred box or tabernacle in which a replica
of the Divine Mirror (enshrined at Ise) was preserved
as the emblem of the Sun-Goddess, when, after being
first stricken by a dazzling radiance which revealed
itself, they finally became demented (*A. K.y.*, Vol. IV,

p. 115).

Very similar to this is what took place in the case of Yahweh's Ark when God's wrath crushed Uzzah to death on his sacrilegious hands touching the divine tabernacle, as we read in *II Samuel* (VI, 6, 7) and *I Chronicles* (XIII, 7–10). The Japanese Divine Mirror and Yahweh's Ark seem originally to have been of the nature of tabooed fetishes.

In the *Nihongi* we find a deity designated "Amatsu-Kagami-no-Mikoto" or the "Heavenly Mirror Augustness," which is the climax of the religious consciousness of worshipping the mirror, *i. e.*, the deification of the mirror.

Therefore, it is quite natural that according to the *Kojiki*, the Great Ancestral Sun-Goddess Amaterasu-Ōmikami gave the Mirror to her grandson Ninigi-no-Mikoto on his descent to earth and ordered him to regard the Mirror as her august soul or spirit and worship it as he was wont to worship her in Heaven (*E. T. K.*, p. 109).

Some jewels have also magical or miraculous powers. The jewels that Watatsumi-no-Kami or Sea-God presented to his heavenly guest and son-in-law, Hikohohodemi-no-Mikoto, in the Royal Dragon Palace, are endowed with supernatural virtues. The Tide-flowing and Tide-ebbing Jewels are nothing but charms or talismans. By shaking them, the possessor of the

Jewels can control at pleasure the rise or fall of the tide of the sea (*E. T. N.*, Vol. 1, p. 100).

Tradition has it that when the Emperor Yōzei, somewhat mentally deranged, opened the lid of the box in which the Yasakani-no-Magatama or Divine Jewels were kept something like white clouds miraculously rose up out of the box to the awful astonishment of the Emperor (*Kojidan*, Vol, I. *K. T.*, Vol. XV, p. 4). The reader may well remember that there is a jewel among the "Ten Sacred Auspicious Treasures" called "Makarukaeshi-no-Tama" or the Jewel of Resuscitating the Dead, which, when shaken, has the miraculous virtue of restoring life to the departed. And so when Susano-o-no-Kami and Amaterasu-Ōmikami exchanged their own treasures and the one shook the jewels while the other shook the sword, on Susano-o-no-Kami's side five male children and on Amaterasu-Ōmikami's side three female children were miraculously born (*E. T. K.*, pp. 47–49). This was chiefly due to the supernatural virtue of the divine sword and jewels. Therefore Imbe-no-Hironari says in his book "Between these two Deities (Amaterasu-Ōmikami and Susano-o-no-Kami) and by virtue of these jewels, the child Akatsu-no-Mikoto was born" (*E. T. Kg.*, p. 18). The same marvelous power was also ascribed to the mirror, when the *Nihongi* tells us that the God Izanagi got two children, the Sun-Goddess and the Moon-God, each time by raising a copper mirror in either hand (*E. T. N.*, Vol. I, p. 20).

The next step to the belief in the possession by the jewel of miraculous virtues is to deify the jewel itself and make a fetish-god of it. Thus, it is said that Akaruhime-no-Kami, the Goddess of the Himekoso Shrine, is a red jewel (*E. T. K.*, p. 259). And in the Divine Age the jewels around the neck of Izanagi-no-Mikoto are deified and called the Deity of Mikuratana or the August-Store-House-Shelf-Deity (*ibid.*, p. 43).

According to another tradition, a stone instead of a jewel was said to be the divine emblem of the Himekoso Shrine (*E. T. N.*, Vol I, p. 168), and so we find the existence of litholatry in ancient Japanese religion. The *Manyōshū* also tells us that there was a stone fetish in the time of the Empress Jingō, in Kyūshū, which she took with her on her expedition to Korea in order that the magical virtue of the stone should delay till her return to Japan birth of the child of which she was enceinte.

Therefore this stone fetish is called the Miharashi-zume-no-Ishi (Chinkaiseki or Guardian Stone of the Empress against untimely childbirth. *Manyōshū*, Vol. v). So in the *Kojiki* we have also a stone completely deified under the name of Chigaeshi-no-Ōkami or the Great Deity who prevented the Goddess Izanami of the Underworld from returning to the upper earth

(*E. T. K.*, p. 38).

The most striking instance of litholatry or worship of stone fetishes is found in a work entitled *Nihon-Montoku-Tennō-Jitsuroku*[1] or *Authentic Japanese History of the Montoku-Tennō Era* (Vol. VIII. *K. T.*, Vol. III, p. 540). According to the narration in that book two stone fetishes one night all of a sudden made their appearance in an effulgence of strange and awful light on the shore of Ōarai, Hitachi Province, in the reign of the Emperor Montoku (827–858), and oracles declared that they were no other than Ōnamuchi-no-Kami and Sukunahikona-no-Kami, both Gods still worshipped at the Ōarai-Isosaki Shrine.

Yamada-no-Sohoto, otherwise called Kuebiko or the Crumbling Prince, which is nothing but a scarecrow set up in rice fields to ward off predatory birds, is a great fetish-god, who "knows anything and everything under the sun, even though it is always kept standing still," according to the *Kojiki* (*E. T. K.*, pp. 86, 87).

According to Amano-Nobukage, a hoe or mattock which ceremoniously cultivates rice plants in the divine fields of the Ise-Jingū is a fetish-god (*Saishi-Zatsui* or *Miscellaneous Collection of Shintō Cults*).

The Deity of the Izukashi Shrine in Awaji is a pair of sandals, which the Emperor Kōmei (1831–1867)

---

1 Or, "Montoku-Jitsuroku" for the sake of brevity.

wore when he worshipped at the Imperial Household
Sanctum called "Kashikodokoro" or "Naishidokoro,"
in charge of the Court Shintō priestesses, where a
special divine mirror, a replica of that of the Ise
Shrine, was enshrined.

The Izukashi Shrine was built by the celebrated
scholar Suzuki-Shigetane and is popularly known as
"Okutsusama" or "the August Imperial Sandals,"
and common people in the locality still believe that
if it is prayed to the pain of diseases will be taken
off, *i.e.*, cured.

Some other fetishes in phallic form, believed to be
endowed with magic virtue, were set up in the rice
fields to propitiate Mitoshi-no-Kami or the Deity of
Rice Crops, according to the *Kogoshūi* account
(*E. T. Kg.*, p. 51). Such phallic emblems were worshipped generally in ancient times, and even now in
secluded parts of the land this practice is credulously
continued. The country folk have been very serious
in believing in the spells of phallic fetishes, which
oftentimes are closely connected with agricultural
Shintō rites performed in Shintō shrines. For example, at the Kinensai or Festival for Praying for
Rich Harvest, a spring Shintō rite of obscene orgiastic
nature, closely connected with the Tagata Shrine in
Higashi-Kasugai-Gun, Owari Province, and another
spring Shintō rite of the same nature in the Hachiman

Shrine of Niike at Fukuchi Village, in Hazu-Gun, Mikawa Province, and a licentious ceremony of cultivating rice in the divine fields of the Warei Shrine in Uwajima, Iyo Province, and that of the Sugiyama Shrine at the Takami Village in Tachibana-Gun, Musashi Province, are all Japanese Dionysian festivals in close connection with agricultural production[1].

Sae-no-Kami, Funado-no-Kami, Dōsojin, Saruta-hiko-no-Ōkami, Ame-no-Uzume-no-Mikoto, Yachimata-hiko, Yachimatahime, and Konsei-Daimyōjin—each of these is a veritable Japanese Priapos, in original Shintō more or less connected with agriculture, although not without some other aspects of divine function from the beginning (*Vide* My essay *A Study of the Development of Religious Ideas among the Japanese People as Illustrated by Japanese Phallicism. T.A.S.J.*, Vol. I, *Supplement.* Dec. 1924).

[1] *Cf.* Martin P. Nilsson, *History of Greek Religion*, p. 91.
E. Washburn Hopkins, *History of Religions*, p. 24.
D. Hans Haas, *Germanische Religion*, 27, 28, 46 (*Bilderatlas zur Religionsgeschichte*).

CHAPTER IV

SPIRITISM

According to the *Nihongi*, in ancient Japan, the people, in their crude philosophy, believed that trees and herbs could speak like men (*E. T. N.* Vol. I, p. 64), and some of the *Norito* or *Shintō Rituals* also mention that there was a belief among the primitive Japanese that rocks, trunks of trees, even tiny blades of herbs are endowed with the power of speech (K. A. Florenz, *Ancient Japanese Rituals. T. A. S. J.*, Vol. XXVII, Part I).

The same animistic conception of Nature displays itself in an account of the funeral in Heaven of the notorious traitor Amewakahiko, when different birds participate, like men, in the ceremony (*E. T. N.*, Vol. I, p. 66). These records furnish evidence that the ancient Japanese consciousness had already reached the stage of animism or polydemonism in the so-called Divine Age, which amounts to saying that the ancient Japanese had a belief in souls or spirits. According to some of the old historical books it is reported that, among the ancient Japanese, there was a belief in four kinds of souls or spirits: the *nigimitama* or gentle spirit, the *aramitama* or rough spirit, the *sakimitama* or luck-spirit, and the *kushimitama* or wondrous spirit. These are not four aspects of one and the same soul or spirit, as most native scholars of the Tokugawa Regime were inclined to interpret, even Moto-ori, the faithful commentator of the *Kojiki*, being disposed to do so, but the actual belief of the ancient Japanese, sharing, in my opinion, the nature of the belief prevailing among primitive peoples generally, which assumes the existence of several kinds of souls or spirits embodied in each individual. So, for example, the ancient Egyptians believed in two kinds of souls, *i.e.*, *ka* and *ba*, the ancient Babylonians *zi* and *lil*, the Chinese *hun* and *p'o*, the Igorot of the Philippines, *taka* (the soul of the living) and *annito* (the soul of the dead), the Ainu *moacha* (the gentle uncle) and *shiacha* (the rough uncle), the Calabar Negroes four souls, just as the ancient Japanese, some aborigines in Borneo and Malay seven souls, the Laos of French Indo-China thirty souls (Stratton, *Psychology of the Religious Life*, p. 267), and so on. According to the *Nihongi*, the God Ōnamuchi had a talk with his own double or *alter ego*, *kushimitama* and *sakimitama*, and the person of the Empress Jingō was guarded by the gentle spirit of the Sea-God while the warships under her command in an expedition to Korea were guided by the rough spirit of the same God.

As regards the nature of the soul or spirit, the

ancient Japanese conception is crude and to a great extent materialistic, as is usually the case among primitive peoples. First of all, the Japanese word "kokoro," soul or spirit, or meaning, rather, both mind and heart, is used quite synonymously in some of the Japanese classical books with the word "hara," which in English means belly. So, in the *Manyōshū*, the poet used the Japanese expression "Mikokoro-o-shizume-tamō," literally, "to calm her mind or heart," meaning "to keep quiet her belly or rather womb," by binding two stones endowed with magic virtues around the body of the Empress Jingō that they might miraculously prevent her from giving birth to a child during her expedition to Korea (*Manyōshū*, Vol. v). In the *Kojiki*, instead of "mind or heart" the word "womb" is used (*E. T. K.*, p. 233). This clearly shows that the ancient Japanese conception of soul or spirit was not quite free from a materialistic aspect. Secondly, the ancient Japanese saw their soul or spirit in the form of light (and later possibly fire), so that the God Ōnamuchi entered into conversation with his *alter ego* or double, the Teutonic *filgja,* the *kushimitama* or wondrous spirit and the *sakimitama* or luck-spirit, on the seashore of Izumo Province, according to the *Nihongi.* A court-lady and poetess, Izumi-Shikibu by name, in the reign of the Emperor Ichijō (985–1011), identified the soul or spirit with the fire-fly (*Jikkinshō,* Vol. III.

K. T., Vol. XV, p. 799). Thirdly, the archaic Japanese "mikage" or "august shadow" means "mitama" or "august soul," so instead of the ordinary expression "Suminoe-no-Aramitama-no-Kami," "Suminoe-no-Aramikage-no-Kami" is used, according to the *Ruiju-Kokushi* (Vol. XVI). Even nowadays at Fuse Village in Himi-Gun, Toyama Prefecture, there is a shrine in memory of the celebrated Ōtomo-no-Yakamochi (*d.* 785), and the shrine is called the Mikage Shrine, meaning the shrine dedicated to the spirit of Ōtomo-no-Yakamochi. Fourthly, the mirror is the soul or spirit, so the ancient Japanese believed, that is to say, the mirror is not a mere emblem of the soul or spirit but is itself a man's soul or spirit. Therefore the ancestral Sun-Goddess, when conferring the Divine Mirror upon her Grandson, said that always when he gazed upon this sacred treasure he would behold in it her divine self, and he must therefore reverently worship it (*Cf. E. T. Kg.*, p. 27, *E. T. N.*, Vol. I, p. 83, *E. T. K.*, p. 109). Fifthly, that the sword is also regarded as a soul or spirit is apparent from the fact that the sword was called "Futsu-no-Mitama" or the "Soul that cuts well" (*E. T. N.*, Vol. I. p. 115). Sixthly, it was almost universally believed in ancient times that the wind is the breath of the universe and one's breath is nothing but a wind in one's own self. Therefore we

have a God of the Wind called Shinatsuhiko, meaning
a "God of Long Breath," as well as the compound
word "tama-shihi"[1] or "Jewel-breath [wind]-fire"
(although this tentative etymological explanation of
mine contradicts Tanikawa-Kotosuga's view given in
his epoch-making work *Wakun-no-Shiori*, a dictionary
of the Japanese language, which barely conveys the
sense of soul or spirit), so that we may safely conclude
that the ancient Japanese conception of soul or spirit
is that of breath, and that to die, *i. e.*, "shinuru" or
"shi-inuru" means "breath-passing-away," in other
words, "soul's leaving one's body." Seventhly, the
ancient Japanese envisage the soul or spirit as something like vapour or smoke or a gray cloud-like
substance. The old legend of Urashima, the Japanese
Rip Van Winkle, tells us that when, on his return
to earth, Urashima opened the casket of longevity
presented him by the beautiful princess of the Dragon-
King under the sea, something like white cloud or
vapour or breath, which was no other than the essence
of his life, *i. e.*, his soul or spirit, flew off high in the
sky and all of a sudden the youthful Urashima became
old and decrepit, and at last passed away. Eighthly,
the ancient Japanese went a step further, and a
shooting star or meteor was popularly known as a
man's soul or spirit (*Fusōryakki*, Vol. XXIV. *K. T.*, Vol.

    [1] Nowadays pronounced "tama-shi-i."

VI, p. 696). Ninthly, a white bird was regarded as a kind of disembodied spirit, so the *Nihongi* mentions that the soul or spirit of Prince Yamatotakeru-no-Mikoto in the form of a white bird[1] ascended to Heaven (*E. T. N.*, Vol. I, p. 217), just like the Egyptian *ba* which, in the shape of a heron, ascends to Heaven. Tenthly, the serpent was believed to be the soul or spirit of the dead, so when the general Tamichi was killed in battle and his grave was being dug by his ferocious Ainu enemy, an incarnation of Tamichi's soul or spirit, in the form of a serpent, appeared from the grave and endeavoured to destroy the foe by whom he had been slain (*E. T. N.*, Vol. I, p. 296).

I have enumerated above the forms of soul or spirit in which the ancient Japanese believed and which the soul or spirit was wont to assume when it manifested itself. Now let us examine what functions such a soul or spirit performs.

A person or natural object, whether animate or inanimate, was believed to be often possessed by a disembodied spirit, and animism was the natural result of this. Consequently, as is shown above, when the Empress Jingō started on her expedition to Korea, the gentle spirit of a god attached itself to the very person of the Empress in order to protect her, while

1 Greek Legend tells us that " the soul of Aristeas flew out of his mouth as a raven " (Martin P. Nilsson, *History of Greek Religion*, p. 102).

the rough spirit of the same god hovered over and guided the Imperial warships (*E. T. N.*, Vol. I, p. 229). In the Divine Age Ame-no-Uzume-no-Mikoto was possessed and inspired by a deity, and the Empress Jingō herself was a divinely inspired person, as well as Ikatsu-no-Omi, who was a "saniwa" or "divine medium" through whom revelations were received. Such divine personages are the shamans of the Mongols, the kiton of the Formosans, the noro of the Loochoo Islanders, the Korean mudang, the Polynesian pia atua ("god-boxes"), etc. In the *Kokon-Chomonshū* (Vol. II), we are informed that a woman was possessed by the Deity of Kasuga and was able to give prompt answers to the most difficult questions put to her by the Buddhist monk Kōben[1] (1163–1222) of Toganō, in Kyōto (*K. T.*, Vol. XV, pp. 207, 208).

In the fire-walking festival of Seki-no-waki in Yama-Gun, Iwashiro, persons possessed by certain local deities, become ecstatic, wave offerings made of paper and wood, and walk barefooted on charcoal fire without injury; they are veritable ἔνθεοι in the true sense of the term; on that occasion of festival, they are, for the moment, entirely beside themselves (Yoshida-Tōgo, *Dainihon-Chimeijisho*, Vol. III, p. 4017).

In order to prevent this spirit from going astray from the body, the Mitamashizume-no-Matsuri (Chin-

[1] Otherwise called Myōe-Shōnin.

konsai) or Spirit-quieting Ceremony was solemnized,
originating from the time of the first human Emperor
Jimmu, the priest being Umashimade-no-Mikoto (*Kuji-
Hongi*, Vol. V. *K. T.*, Vol. VII, pp. 264, 321, 322).

According to the *Sōsōryō* or *Administrative Law
of the Funeral of the Dead*, there were specialists
called Asobi-Be under whose sole care the ceremony
of appeasement of the anger of evil spirits was conducted (*Ryō-no-Shūge*, Vol. IV).

If the influence that a distant spirit has upon a
person is termed obsession, a similar function may
be observed in punishment by tatari or divine curse.
For instance, according to the *Kogoshūi,* when the
peasants acted against the will of Mitoshi-no-Kami,
the Deity of Rice Crops, clouds of locusts were, as a
divine curse, sent by the wrathful Deity to destroy
the young rice plants in the rice fields of the offenders
(*E. T. Kg.*, pp. 48, 49). According to the *Nihongi*, the
Emperor Ingyō suffered a great deal from a curse of
the Deity of Awaji Island, because he failed to make
sacrifice to it of a great sea-ear[1] (*E. T. N.*, Vol. I, p. 323).

The Emperor Temmu (622–686) fell sick under a
curse of the Deity of the Kusanagi Sword, according
to the *Nihongi.* And Ōmononushi-no-Kami of Izumo
frequently, in wrathful divine mood, delivered curses
on the Imperial Court of Yamato.

[1] Haliotis tuberculata.

Such curses, in the form of punishment upon offenders, may be called a divine function of obsession, and at the same time divine favour or unseen and yet actual protection from Heaven may likewise be so termed. Hence the Emperor Jimmu or the Empress Jingō conducted their expeditions under the unseen protection of the Ancestral Sun-Goddess and other deities.

The divine will was often revealed in a dream; divine oracles could be heard. Thus it is recorded that during his campaigns the Emperor Jimmu received the revelations of the Sun-Goddess in dreams, as mentioned in the *Nihongi*, and in a dream by the Emperor Yūryaku the Ancestral Sun-Goddess revealed her desire that the Food-Goddess Toyouke-Daijin should be invited from Tamba Province to serve her as divine waitress at the Inner Shrine of Ise—which desire was duly executed.

In order to ascertain the divine will, divination is very common among the ancient Japanese, and tradition tells us that matters connected with it were controlled in Heaven by Ame-no-Koyane-no-Mikoto (*E. T. N.*, Vol. I, p. 83). In ancient times divination was performed by taking note of how the shoulder-blade of a deer cracks when exposed to fire. Afterwards, influenced by Chinese methods, the shell of a tortoise was employed. In his book entitled *Seibokukō* or *Notes on Genuine Divination* Ban-Nobutomo mentions several methods which I cannot well refer to here.

Holding steadfastly to the unseen power of the Divine, the ancient Japanese believed in ordeal or divine judgment. For example, the reader may be familiar with the "Kugadachi" or boiling water ordeal —"saimon" among the Ainu—and the fire ordeal of the ancient Japanese. An instance of the former is found in the reign of the Emperor Ingyō (*E. T. N.*, Vol. I, p. 316. *Shinsen-Shōjiroku-Kōshō, Preface*) and of the latter there is the legend of Konohana-no-Sakuyahime, the Flowery Goddess of Beauty, when she undertook to prove her innocence of her husband's groundless accusation of adultery, just as did Yaśodharā, wife of Siddārtha, or Sītā, wife of Rāma, the Indian hero of the *Rāmāyana* (*Vide* Dutt, *Rāmāyana* [English translation], pp. 162–164. Griffith, *Rāmāyana* [English translation], v, 277. *Zappōzōkyō* or *Saṁyuktaratnapitaka-Sūtra.* Nanjiō's *Catalogue*, No. 1329).

As men and women lived and moved and had their being under the supervision of the deities, the ancient Japanese very often took oath by one or other of their deities. So it is noteworthy that in the Divine Age Amaterasu-Ōmikami and Susano-o-no-Mikoto gave birth to children by oath.

When a man's soul leaves his body, death follows,

so the ancient Japanese believed. Therefore at the death of Amewakahiko, his relations and friends "disported themselves for eight days and eight nights." in order that thereby they might recall his temporarily absent soul to its original body (*E. T. N.*, Vol. I, pp. 66, 67. *E. T. K.*, p. 98).

The ancient Japanese thought that the dead have a consciousness; that this belief once actually existed can be proved by the tradition that the soul of Tamichi, the ancient brave warrior of Japan, when he was killed in battle by the strong hostile troops of the Emishi or Ainu, never lost its consciousness, even though his body perished (*E. T. N.*, Vol I, p. 296). The conscious dead, so far still alive, has need of his servants, horses, weapons, and so on, just as in his lifetime; consequently, we have the so-called "junshi" or servants accompanying their master in death to the Underworld by being entombed along with his corpse—a horrible custom that was prohibited by an Edict of the Emperor Kōtoku in the year 646, when the Emperor had the administrative organization of the Empire revised. Such being the case, the grave is a place where the soul or spirit of the dead resides, and so far, in case the dead are deified, the grave *de facto* can be turned to a shrine where the divine spirit, which is a god, is to be worshipped. Therefore we have the old song :—

"Sweet solace follows me
Since kneeling by the stone,
And offering prayers to him
Who reigneth there alone"
(*Vide* Tachibana-no-Moribe, *Kagurauta-Iriaya*, Vol. II.
Collected Works, Vol. VII. pp. 43, 44).

In Iyo Province, as early as 878, we had the
"Deity at the Grave" (*Nihon-Sandai-Jitsuroku*,[1] Vol.
XXXIV. *K. T.*, Vol. IV, p. 494), and tradition says that
when the Goddess Izanami was killed by the Fire-
God Kagutsuchi, she was buried in Arima Village,
Kii Province, being worshipped with offerings of
flowers and banners flying, while, in front of the
grave, votaries danced and sang to the music of flutes
and drums (*E. T. N.*, Vol. I, pp. 21, 22). Even nowadays we can readily trace, in certain localities, shrines
that have been transformed from what were originally
graves. For example, the Inu Shrine[2] of Izumo,
dedicated to Ame-no-Mikatsuhime-no-Mikoto in remote
antiquity, is nothing but a himorogi or sacred tree
planted on a round mound, which is neither more nor
less than an ancient tumulus. The case is the same
with the Shrine of Konda Hachiman in Kawachi.

So it may be fairly safe to say that one of the
origins of a Shintō shrine is the grave where the

1 Or, briefly, "Sandai-Jitsuroku."
2 The shrine is mentioned in the *Izumofudoki* or *Ancient Topography of Izumo Province.*

ancient dead found a last resting place.

Now let us consider what is the place to which the dead proceed. The land of the dead is called "Yomi-no-Kuni," meaning "Yami-no-Kuni" or the land of darkness, or "Tokoyo-no-Kuni" or the land of eternal night. The land of darkness, the Japanese Sheol or Hades, is a region, gloomy, filthy and polluted, situated at the remotest corner beneath the earth, as the ancient Japanese believed. Being filthy and polluted, visitors necessarily require, on their return from it, to cleanse themselves in lustral waters, as, according to tradition, Izanagi purified his contaminated body after he had visited the Underworld. Therefore, to the ancient Japanese, death is a pollution, so that even utterance of the words "death" and "grave" is to be avoided in the holy precincts of Ise Shrine (*Kōtaijingū-Gishikichō. G. R. k.*, Vol. I, p. 4).

Moto-ori-Norinaga, wishing to be very faithful to the original meaning of the *Kojiki* and *Nihongi* myths, says :—

"Oh! that for myriad years I might this life retain
    Ere doomed to dwell in death's polluted dark
                            domain."

As mentioned above, the so-called Tokoyo-no-Kuni literally means the land of eternal night, *i. e.*, the land where utter darkness eternally prevails. This is probably the first or original meaning of the word

"Tokoyo-no-Kuni," I presume. But by degrees that conception has passed into a second interpretation of the word: namely, the land of eternity, *i. e.*, the Region of Eternal Bliss where the inhabitants know no death, or Paradise; and this idea again leads us to the realm of Takama-ga-Hara or the Plain of High Heaven, which is the abode of the celestial beings of Shintō, this rendering being greatly promoted by Taoist ideas from China in which, among other things, for instance, the mythical Mt. Hōrai (P'êng Lai), the Land of Eternity or Eternal Bliss, becomes an ideal land, where the sennin or Taoistic mythical beings dwell. Thirdly the word may be taken as indicating a land far, very far, distant from Japan, not altogether in the beyond but somewhere yet on the hither side of earth.

Of these three renderings of the word "Tokoyo-no-Kuni," that of Paradise is closely related to Takama-ga-Hara or the Plain of High Heaven, where the Shintō deities dwell. The Plain of High Heaven is an ideal celestial region, the Japanese Olympos, to which the souls of the dead of high ranks, not of common mortals, are believed to ascend in a similar way, as the Sun-Goddess and the Moon-God, who, though born on earth, were sent up to the Plain of High Heaven by their Divine Parents Izanagi and Izanami, or Izanagi himself returned to Heaven when he had fulfilled his commissioned duties in this world. It is the brilliant ethereal domain of the glorious sun, while this land of Yamato or Japan is where the sun was born,—Nihon or Nippon meaning the birth place or cradle of the sun—and so Japan is a land of light, a realm of brightness, a place of endless sunshine, in short, Akitsukuni or Akitsushima, diametrically opposed to the Yomi-no-Kuni or Land of Eternal Darkness, the Underworld or Hades, entirely regardless of or putting aside the false traditional meaning attached to the word "Akitsushima", derived from its resemblance on the map to the shape of a dragon fly. It is believed that the spirits of sovereigns, and princes, warriors for the most part, soar to Heaven or the Plain of High Heaven, while those of ordinary common mortals sink to Hades. So both this earthly Nippon and the ideal celestial region enjoy forever the brilliance of the sun ; while entirely devoid of light is the Underworld, a hideous polluted land where gloomy darkness prevails eternally. This is the reason why the Japanese of all times cherish and adhere to this glorious land of their birth, never, as did the ancient Hindu, looking for an ideal beyond but rather, on the contrary, recoiling from any thought of wandering elsewhere. It is a remarkable fact which the student may well remember that herein lies one of the fundamental differences of religious thought between the Japanese

and the Chinese, because in China from time im-
memorial Heaven itself is a God, very often personified
as Shangti or the Supreme Ruler, while in Japan
Takama-ga-Hara or the Plain of High Heaven (*i. e.,*
Heaven) is no other than the abode of the deities,
Heaven itself never being a divinity. To our great
surprise, however, in the reigns of the Emperors
Kammu (782–805) and Montoku (851–858), owing to
the influence of Chinese culture then flourishing in
Japan, it seems that Heaven Itself was actually wor-
shipped at Katano, Kawachi Province (*Shoku-Nihongi*,
Vols. XXXVIII, XXXIX. *K. T.*, Vol. II, pp. 720, 735. *Nihon-
Montoku-Tennō-Jitsuroku*, Vol. VIII. *K. T.*, Vol. III, p. 539).
This shows how Japanese minds were then particularly
affected by the powerful influence of Chinese culture.

CHAPTER V

Anthropolatry and Ancestor Worship in the Stage of Nature Religion

I Primitive Anthropolatry

In Japan examples of anthropolatry or worship of divine personages are too numerous to count. In the following lines we shall deal with this subject from two different sides, viz., the worship of man while living, on one hand, and the same worship after death, on the other.

In ancient Japan the Emperor and Empress are Kami or deities even in their lifetimes. So, for instance, the Emperor Jimmu was called the Ame-no-Oshigami or Conquering-Deity of Heaven, as Aston put it in English (*E. T. N.*, Vol. I, p. 125), and the Empress Jingō was also a Goddess to the eye of a poet of the *Manyōshū*, when he says :—

"With reverential awe Thy name I breathe,
Goddess Divine, Tarashihime!"[1]

(*Manyōshū*, Vol. V)

In the *Kojiki* she is called a deity by one of her warriors at the time of the conquest of Korea. The

[1] Another name for the Empress Jingō. Properly, Okinaga-Tarashihime.

learned Moto-ori thinks that she is thus spoken of because, being possessed of the deities, she is a deity herself (*E. T. K.*, p. 230).

In several old Japanese histories the following expression frequently occurs : "The Emperor, as God Incarnate, rules over the Great-Eight-Island-Country,"[1] indicating clearly the belief that the Emperor is a human manifestation of the Divine.

The Emperor Keikō was also termed "A Deity visible of men," which I take to mean something like an incarnate God, a God that can be seen by men—*Vide* the following passage from the *Nihongi* :—

"The Prince[2] answered and said :—'I am the son of a Deity[3] visible of men.' Hereupon the Yemishi were all filled with Awe" (*E. T. N.*, vol. I, p. 206).

According to the *Fusōryakki*, written by the Buddhist priest Kōen, venerable master of the celebrated Buddhist monk Hōnen (1133–1221), founder of the Jōdo Sect, a veteran warrior Minamoto-no-Yoshiie was so strong and courageous as to be regarded even by his enemies as a divinity—a human-god, a *Deus-Homo*. In the history entitled *Mizukagami* another famous warrior, Sakanoue-no-Tamuramaro, also, was looked up to not as an ordinary man but an extraordinary one, *i. e.*, a superhuman being (*N. B. Z. h.*, vol.

1 *I. e.*, Japan.
2 Yamatotakeru.
3 The Emperor Keikō.

XXIII, p. 130. Saga-Tennō, *Tamuramaro-Denki* in *G. R. k.*, Vol. IV, p. 362).

The case mentioned in the *Mizukagami* is similar to that of the Spartan general Lysandros, and of Alexander the Great. The two oriental warriors, Minamoto-no-Yoshiie and Sakanoue-no-Tamuramaro, like Lysandros, were deified even in their lifetimes[1].

Yamazaki-Ansai (1618–1682), a well-known scholar of Chinese classics, built a shrine called "Suika-Reisha" in honour of his own divine spirit, just as Ōnamuchi-no-Kami did on Mt. Miwa in Yamato Province during the Divine Age (*E. T. N.*, Vol. I, p. 61).

The Ōhafuri or High Shintō Priests attached to the Shrine of Suwa in Shinano Province and those High Priests of Iyo Province under whose superintendence was placed the Shrine of Ōyamatsumi-no-Kami or the God of the Mountain were looked up to as living gods in human form. Moreover, every year the High Shintō Priest of the Suwa Shrine was worshipped with animal sacrifices—seventy-five deer-heads—just as Demetrios Poliorketes, when he restored the Athenian democracy in 307 B. C., enjoyed the fame of a living god and was worshipped with due religious ceremony (Chantepie de la Saussaye, *Lehrbuch der Religionsgeschichte*, 3. Aufl., Bd. II, S. 402. Sir J. Frazer, *Magical Origin of Kings*, pp. 137, 138).

---

1 *Cf.* G. Murray, *Five Stages of Greek Religion*, p. 189.

Examples of worship of a man after death are rather numerous: Japan is a classical land of necrolatry or worship of the spirit of the dead and of ancestor worship, *i. e*, worship of the spirit of the dead ancestor. Several of the mausolea of the Emperors are after all Shintō shrines, and people repair to them to worship the august spirits of the dead Emperors. Needless to cite as an instance the worship at the Momoyama Mausolea of the Emperor Meiji (1852–1912) and the Empress Shōken (1850–1914), which well illustrates our case. Moreover, the Tenjin of Dazaifu in Kyūshū and that of Kitano in Kyōto represent the hero Sugawara-no-Michizane (845–903), deified after his lamented death. Tokugawa-Ieyasu (1542–1616), the founder of the Tokugawa Shogunate, was deified, at his death, as the Tōshōdaigongen or East-Shining-Great-Divine-Hero, and his tomb at Nikkō is an object of worship, while his rival opponent and predecessor Toyotomi-Hideyoshi (1536–1598) was deified in the same way and his tomb at Amidagamine in Kyōto is nothing less than a shrine to the minds of worshippers there. The case is the same with the Tanzan Shrine in Yamato Province, which originally was the tomb of Fujiwara-no-Kamatari[1] (*d.* 669). The Shrine of the God Konda Hachiman in Kawachi also originated in all probabil-

---

[1] Some Japanese historians hold the opinion that this is not the tomb of Kamatari, but of Fujiwara-no-Fuhito, his son.

ity, from the grave of the Emperor Ōjin.

The Akina Shrine on the Kamo River in Kyôto is a shrine dedicated to the dead ancestors of the Mitsui family—a family of rich Japanese merchants of world-wide fame—from generation to generation, although each paterfamilias on decease was provisionally interred with Buddhist rites and, after the lapse of years, was wont to be canonized Shintoistically, so to speak, in the Akina Shrine.

II ANCESTOR WORSHIP IN ANCIENT JAPAN

Now let us pass on to the study of ancestor worship in ancient Japan. Some authorities affirm that Japanese religion originated from ancestor worship while others deny this and insist instead that it was nature worship that made the beginning of Japanese religion and that the ancestor worship of the Japanese was imported from China long after the introduction of Confucianism into Japan. Among the foreign authorities Lafcadio Hearn is an advocate of the former view while W. G. Aston advanced the latter theory, whereas M. Revon and P. Lowell hold a syncretic view-point standing between the two antagonistic parties. The ancestor worship theory explaining the origin of Japanese religion was very popular among native scholars of the Tokugawa Regime and they held it as nearly self-evident, while, on the contrary,

Aston ascribed the origin of Japanese ancestor worship to Chinese influence on religious thought. According to Aston, Amaterasu-Ōmikami is a deification of the sun and nothing else, never an ancestral deity in its origin in the true sense of the term. The worship of Amaterasu-Ōmikami is indeed a pseudo-ancestor worship. I belong to neither of the parties mentioned above—believing that the truth lies in neither extreme, but in the golden mean. I am of opinion that the origin of Japanese religion partakes of both nature worship and ancestor worship; the two elements being mingled together. Who can prove with historical certainty that ancestor worship is utterly absent in ancient Japan? Of old we have some heroines in Japan, for example, the Empress Jingō who in person led the Japanese army to Korea, and the famous Himiko of Tsukushi (Kyūshū) who ruled over that locality, mentioned in the *Gishi* (*Wei Chi*) or *History of Gi* (*Wajinden* or *History of the Japanese*) written by Chinju (Ch'ên Shou) of West Shin (Hsi Chin) in the third century. In like manner it is possible that ancient Japan had a female sovereign, Amaterasu-Ōmikami by name, like the Empress Jingō or Himiko of Tsukushi, and whose political career was inseparably connected with solar myths in so remote a mythical age. So understood, it may be not unreasonable to consider Amaterasu-Ōmikami as partly mythological (the solar myths as ascribed to her in the *Kojiki* and the *Nihongi*) and partly historical. Not all of the *Kojiki*, the *Nihongi* and the *Kogoshūi* narrations are purely mythological, or wholly lacking in historical significance ; on the contrary, it is quite certain that they furnish historical materials of ancient Japan, though they were not compiled in book form until the eighth and ninth centuries.

There Amaterasu-Ōmikami has indeed an aspect of a solar deity and yet at the same time it is possible that she has an aspect of the great ancestral deity from whom the Japanese Imperial family are sprung.

Next let us proceed a step further and consider the time when Japanese ancestor worship in the course of history actually existed. With a little digression here, first of all, we must note that while the *Kojiki*,[1] the *Nihongi*,[2] the *Kogoshūi*[3] and the *Takahashi-Ujibumi*,[4] were compiled as books only in the eighth century or later, their materials are of quite ancient origin, and therefore through these ancient materials we may be able to have some glimpses of religious Japan of old.

Now, returning to our main course of argument, let us first of all consider that the Japanese people

[1] Compiled in 712.
[2] Compiled in 720.
[3] Compiled in 807.
[4] Written in about 757.

at the time of Jimmu-Tennō, the first human Emperor
of Japan, had an ancestor worship, because Ame-no-
Tomi-no-Mikoto, ancestor of the Imbe family, built a
shrine—the present Awa Jinja—in commemoration of
his ancestor Ame-no-Futotama-no-Mikoto, in Bōshū,
in order to worship his Ancestral Deity there, as
Ame-no-Tomi-no-Mikoto and his family were wont to
do before they settled in Bōshū, coming in migration
from Awa in Shikoku. This historical or semi-
historical fact proves that the Japanese people had a
belief in their ancestral deities, taking it for granted
that Ame-no-Futotama-no-Mikoto may be a pseudo-
ancestor of the Imbe family, as Aston presumes; it
amounts to saying that Japanese ancestor worship
actually existed in so early a period as that of
Jimmu-Tennō, the historical founder of the Japanese
Empire (*E. T. Kg.*, p. 32. *Cf.* the *Takahashi-Ujibumi.*
Ban-Nobutomo, *Collected Works*, Vol. III).

Second, in the *Engishiki* or *Institutes of the Engi
Period* (901–923), we find the Kokusō-Jinja of Aso, a
shrine dedicated to a local lord of Aso Province, and
here question arises as to when and in whose memory
that shrine was first erected?

According to the *Kujiki* we are informed that in
the reign of the Emperor Sujin, Hayamikatama-no-
Mikoto, great-grandson of the Emperor Jimmu, was
appointed the first local .lord of Aso Province (*Vide*

Kokusō-Hongi. K. T., Vol. VII, p. 425).

From what is stated above, we can surmise with some probability that the shrine mentioned in the *Engishiki,* as dedicated to a local lord of Aso Province, may be a shrine erected in memory of Hayamikata-no-Mikoto by his descendants when he died, or we may advance another hypothesis, similar to this, that the Kokusō Shrine is a shrine dedicated by Hayamikatama-no-Mikoto himself to his ancestor or ancestors. In either case we have some historical reason to conclude that the Japanese even at so remote a . period as the reign of the Emperor Sujin had a form of ancestor worship, historically almost free from Chinese literary influences.

Third, in the reign of the Emperor Keikō, according to the *Takahashi-Ujibumi,* Mutsukari-no-Mikoto, one of the Imperial princes of Keikō-Tennō, died, during his sojourn in Bōshū, accompanying His Majesty in attendance there. At the death of the beloved Imperial Prince, in commemoration of his meritorious services in cookery to the Emperor, His Majesty built a shrine in the Imperial Palace and dedicated it to the Prince, who became a tutelary god of the Imperial cookery (*Takahashi-Ujibumi. Vide* Ban-Nobutomo, *Collected Works,* Vol. III, pp. 73, 74–107).

This Prince Mutsukari being the ancestor of the Takahashi family, his apotheosis is nothing but an ancestor worship so far as the Takahashi family is concerned. So here we are met with an ancestor worship independent of Chinese literary influences. Needless to say, all these above-mentioned three cases of ancestor worship could not but be free from Chinese influences imported into Japan in the wake of the Korean expedition of the Empress Jingō, because they antedated that expedition. Let us add one more example which runs as follows :

In the reign of the Emperor Sujin a virulent pestilence subsided when the God Ōmononushi was worshipfully prayed to by His divine son Ōtataneko himself, in accordance with divine revelation so to do made in an awe-striking dream by the Emperor (*E. T. N.*, Vol. I, p. 153).

In this case, according to the *Nihongi*, the divine descendant Ōtataneko simply practised ancestor worship, although his divine father Ōmononushi may have been a pseudo-ancestor, as Aston might say. Such an idea cannot appear, unless some form or other of ancestor worship had already existed and formed part of the faith of the ancient Japanese ; in other words, we think we have a good reason to believe that the Japanese people in the Emperor Sujin's reign had had an ancestor worship never derived from Chinese literary sources. We must remember that the earlier parts of the *Kojiki* and the

Nihongi ars full of such passages referring to ancestor worship. To cite two examples out of many: the Emperor Jimmu received unseen protections from his Ancestral Goddess Amaterasu-Ōmikami during his campaigns in the Yamato district, while the tradition —as one might call it—of the Imperial Edict of the Sun-Goddess conferred upon the Heavenly Grandson in his descent to earth could not exist even as a tradition but for the belief of ancestor worship among the ancient Japanese.

We have already seen that necrolatry existed in ancient Japan, and, as necrolatry is a worship of the dead in general, if descendants are to have a worship of their dead ancestors as a necrolatry, in that case a form of ancestor worship naturally comes to pass.

Moreover, as we shall see later on, the theanthropic religious consciousness of the Japanese developed their religion into an ancestor worship, which may reasonably be called a special aspect of theanthropic religion in general.

CHAPTER VI

TOTEMISM AND PRIMITIVE MONOTHEISM IN ORIGINAL SHINTŌ

I SOME TRACES OF THE EXISTENCE OF TOTEMISM IN ANCIENT JAPAN

In my opinion totemism may be considered from two different standpoints, namely, zoolatry (or theriolatry) and ancestor worship. In other words, totemism is a combination of zoolatry and ancestor worship. Totemism holds that a whole clan or an individual person is descended from a certain kindred animal or plant or, very rarely, a certain inorganic object, while the clan or the individual worships such a class of organic or inorganic objects as divine. So totemism I wish to define as follows:—It is a form of worship of some species of animal or plant or, very rarely, a certain inorganic object, such as rain, rock, the sun, etc., which is believed to be a divine progenitor of the clan or of an individual.

Totemism thus defined, let us try to discover traces of its existence at one time in ancient Japan.

According to the *Kojiki* and *Nihongi* myths, Toyotamahime, daughter of the Sea-God, is wife of Hikohohodemi-no-Mikoto, the great-grandson of the

Sun-Goddess Amaterasu-Ōmikami, and by her Hiko-hohodemi-no-Mikoto begot Ugayafukiaezu-no-Mikoto, father of Jimmu-Tennō, from whom it is believed the present Imperial family have descended—the lineage continuing unbrokenly. Toyotamahime, when giving birth to her son, Ugayafukiaezu-no-Mikoto, was transformed into a crocodile, according to one of the old traditions. Moreover, in old traditions of Japan the crocodile is called a deity—"Sabimochi-no-Kami" or the "God of Sabimochi" by name in the *Kojiki* tradition (*E. T. K.*, p. 125)—and was worshipped as a "heavenly crocodile" by a certain Kuhao, according to the documentary fragments of the *Ancient Topography of Settsu Province* (Kurita, *Kofudoki-Itsu-bunkōshō*, Vol. I, p. 47).

Judging from what I have mentioned above, we can conclude with some probability that there may have been a totemic belief among the ancient Japanese, which amounts to saying that the ancient Japanese people had a crocodile totem.

According to ancient traditions, Kamotaketsu-numi-no-Mikoto, ancestor of Kamo-no-Agatanushi and god to whom the Kamo Shrine is dedicated in Kyōto, is reported to have been a large divine crow, who served as faithful guide to the Emperor Jimmu when the latter led his troops against his enemy in the Yamato district, and afterwards, in the year

705, during the reign of the Emperor Mommu, a shrine was dedicated to this divine crow in Uda-Gun, Yamato Province (*Shoku-Nihongi*, Vol. III. *K. T.*, Vol. II, p. 36).

Here we can see that in ancient times there were some people in Japan who deemed themselves as descendants of a divine crow, and in consequence we can conclude that there was a crow totem in ancient Japan.

It may be remembered that at Itsukushima in Aki Province and at Kumano in Kii Province superstitious local people even nowadays very often speak of the divine crows that live in those districts.

Let us proceed a step further and take up the view that some inorganic objects can become totems, then we can add the Sun another typical example of totemism in the Japanese religion, as the Incas revered the Sun as their totem, because the Japanese regarded the Sun as a deity and deemed it the divine ancestress of the Japanese Imperial family.

It goes without saying that the Ainu, the aboriginal people of Japan, had also a totemism in their well-known bear-festival and in their belief in the divine owl, eagle, wolf, and dolphin, as the Rev. Dr. Batchelor and Dr. Kyōsuke Kindaichi of the Tōkyō Imperial University have shown in their writings respectively.

II Deity of Primitive Monotheism in Shintō

Since Andrew Lang's theory of primitive monotheism was brought to light, we have been well acquainted with a belief in some comparatively Great Beings among nature peoples of a lower grade of culture. The Australian Darumulun (Lord, Father) and Munganngaur (Our Father), the Andamanese Puluga, Cagn of the Bushmen, Huillhuembo (Creator) of the Araucanos, and Nyankupon of West Africa are divinities of the so-called primitive monotheism. Pachacamac (Creator) of the Incas and Dingira or Dimir of the ancient Babylonians also belong to the same category.

With a little digression let us add that Dr. Underwood has given in his book *Religions of Eastern Asia*[1] the name of the Korean Supreme God Wanin whom he considers the greatest God of the primitive monotheism of old Korea, but on a closer examination we have found that Wanin is not a deity of Korean origin at all; on the contrary, He is nothing but a Buddhistic God of Vedic origin, *i. e.*, Śakradevanam Indra by name, whom the Buddhist priest Ichi-nen mentioned in his book *Sangokuiji.*

In the Japanese Pantheon of old we can find such

[1] pp. 105, 106.

a comparatively Great Being dimly existing in the Deity called Ame-no-Minakanushi-no-Kami or the Divine Lord of the Very Centre of Heaven. We have good reasons to believe from the standpoint of a comparative study of religion that Ame-no-Minakanushi-no-Kami is really the Deity of Japanese primitive monotheism, and I made public my own view on this point in detail in a paper published in the *Transactions of the Asiatic Society of Japan* nearly two decades ago, which the reader may do well to consult. I shall here only summarize the result of my studies in Ame-no-Minakanushi-no-Kami.

First of all in the *Kojiki* and *Nihongi* myths no special anthropomorphic activities of Ame-no-Minakanushi-no-Kami are mentioned at all while the Divine Couple Izanagi and Izanami, the Sun-Goddess Amaterasu-Ōmikami, the Moon-God Tsukuyomi-no-Mikoto and the Storm-God Susano-o-no-Mikoto are very popular and thoroughly clad in mythical garments of gorgeous colours.

Second, in the *Nihongi* the name of Ame-no-Minakanushi-no-Kami is mentioned once, and once only, in a single account. According to the *Kojiki*, Ame-no-Minakanushi-no-Kami is self-born, not of his parents, with neither wife nor children. The Deity is all self-created in the Takama-ga-Hara or Plain of High Heaven in the beginning. The author of the

Shinsen-Kisōki[1] speaks of the Deity nearly in the same way as does the *Nihongi* (*Cf. E. T. N.*, Vol. I, p. 5).

Third, in the *Kojiki* Ame-no-Minakanushi-no-Kami forms a triad with the two other Musubi-no-Kami or Producing Deities—the High August Producer and the Divine August Producer—and although both Producing Deities or the Divine Producers played an important active rôle in the performances of the heavenly drama of the Divine Age, Ame-no-Minakanushi-no-Kami ever remained inactive. Similarly the Araucanos have a belief in their Supreme Being in a dim existence, the pale Huillhuembo, the Creator of the universe, and yet their actual worship is directed to two of his attributes, Huillpapilbo (Almighty Power) and Moloquechigeln[2] (Eternity). And Nyankupon of West Africa is ignored rather than worshipped, while its deputy God Bobowissi has priests and offerings, as we are informed of by A. Lang.[3]

Fourth, it is quite noteworthy that there is anciently no authentic shrine dedicated to Ame-no-Minakanushi-no-Kami ; not a single shrine erected to him is mentioned in the *Engishiki*. Those shrines

---

[1] This book was compiled in its present form between 830-973 and is preserved in the House of Viscount Yoshida of Kyōto whose ancestors were hereditary Shintō priests.

[2] *Vide* Gybbon Spilsburg's description of the South American tribes in the *Transactions of the History of Religions*, Vol. I, pp. 92, 93.

[3] A. Lang, *Making of Religion*, p. 227.

that are said to have been erected to this Deity are all of later origin.

Fifth, Ame-no-Minakanushi-no-Kami is the Divine Lord of the Very Centre of Heaven, judging from the very signification of the name. How lofty a designation of the Deity! And yet it is a remarkable fact that he plays practically little or no part in the various scenes of the heavenly drama in the *Kojiki* and *Nihongi* myths. Later on he gave way to another Great Being called Kuni-Tokotachi-no-Mikoto or the Earthly Eternal Divine Being—Why? Because the Deity himself belongs to primitive monotheism—to adopt Lang's terminology.

Some native scholars hold the opinion that the God Ame-no-Minakanushi was a later fabrication in Japan by the Japanese for themselves when they became familiar with Chinese culture, making use of the Chinese religious idea of Shangti or the Chinese Lord on high, but this point of argument may not seem quite convincing, from the historical view-point; it seems to lack a complete historical ground; some sceptical critics might say it is only an imagination. Yet who can prove this hypothesis in the affirmative, without any shadow of doubt?

Taking into consideration the belief in those supreme gods of different peoples mentioned above, not only among nature peoples of to-day in a stage of primitive culture, but also among some peoples of ancient times, if we think over what Ame-no-Mina-kanushi-no-Kami is in the traditions of ancient Japan, we can with some degree of probability conclude that Ame-no-Minakanushi-no-Kami is the God of the so-called primitive monotheism indigenous to the soil of Japan and we find little or no trace of importation from China of such monotheism, nor do we find any trace of artificial invention from scholarly or priestly minds as some investigators arbitrarily and dogmatic-ally assume. Such a scholarly invention of divinity we find in Ame-Yuzuru-Hi-Ame-no-Sagiri-Kuni-Yuzuru-Tsuki-Kuni-no-Sagiri-no-Mikoto(=Sun+Moon+Heav-enly Mist+Earthly Mist[1]), a Deity mentioned in the *Kujiki* taking the place of Ame-no-Minakanushi-no-Kami of the *Kojiki* (*K. T.*, vol. VII, p. 173), somewhat similar in construction to the later Persian Divinity Zervanem Akaranem, a personification of infinite time, and the unifying principle of Ahura Mazda and Ahriman, the Supreme Unity of the dualism of the Gods of good and evil in the Sassanian Dynasty (D'Alviella, *Hibbert Lectures on the Origin and Growth of the Conception of God*, p. 226. Cumont, *Oriental Religions in Roman Paganism; the Mysteries of Mithra*, p. 150).

[1] All these prototypes are found in the names of the deities in the *Kojiki. Vide E. T. K.*, p. 28. *Vide* Chapter XII.

Section II Polytheistic Aspect
of Shintō

The polytheistic aspect of Shintō culminates in the description of divine activities during the Divine Age given in the *Kojiki* and the *Nihongi*. The Deities Izanagi and Izanami as husband and wife are chief progenitors in procreating the mountains, rivers, trees and herbs, the Great-Eight-Island-Country as well as the gods and goddesses.

Among the divinities born of the Divine Couple Izanagi and Izanami were Amaterasu-Ōmikami the Sun-Goddess, Tsukuyomi-no-Mikoto the Moon-God, and Susano-o-no-Mikoto the Impetuous Storm-God, these being termed the "Three Noble Children"; the Sun-Goddess of a soft and gentle character ruling over the Plain of High Heaven, the boisterous Storm-God Susano-o reigning over the sea, according to one of the old traditions, while the Moon-God was in charge of the Realm of night. Then came a conflict between the sun and the rainstorm, and the Sun-Goddess attacked by the mischievous God of the Rainstorm was greatly incensed and concealed herself in the Heavenly Rock-Cave. In the long run the Sun-Goddess secured a final victory and, by decision of a council of the heavenly deities, the Storm-God was banished from Heaven to the Underworld or the Izumo district.

On this sentence of banishment the God Susano-o had a farewell interview in the Plain of High Heaven with his sister Amaterasu-Ōmikami, when brother and sister, through an oath of miraculous virtue, gave birth to eight children. In the upper reaches of the River Hi, in Izumo, God Susano-o rescued a maiden named Kushinadahime from a monster serpent with eight heads, which he killed, and subsequently he married the maiden, as Jason, a hero of Greek mythology, took the maiden Medea to wife.

Then the *Kojiki* and *Nihongi* myths bring us to another great scene of the divine drama, where came to pass a new remarkable phase of conflicts between the sky-people who arrived in Tsukushi anew and the older branch of the same stock that had hitherto inhabited the land of Izumo.

Ōkuninushi-no-Kami, the Great Divine Lord of Izumo Province, who is said to be a descendant of the God Susano-o, handed over the governing authority of the whole land to the Heavenly Grandson Ninigi-no-Mikoto, retiring from the active political arena, and retaining charge only of things religious. And, matters thus settled, the Heavenly Grandson made a descent from Heaven to earth and lived in Tsukushi, some time passing before the first human Emperor Jimmu ascended the Throne and subjugated the Yamato district. Then came to an end the Divine Age of the *Kojiki* and the *Nihongi*.

Now let us examine a little more closely by what sort of divine beings the above-mentioned heavenly drama was performed and how Shintō developed itself from polydemonism to polytheism in the true sense of the latter term.

CHAPTER VII

SHINTŌ AS A SHEER POLYTHEISM

In the polytheistic stage of religious development, religion differentiates itself, according to the difference of nationality or mental characteristics of nations, into the monolatry of the ancient Hebrews, the henotheism or kathenotheism of Vedic India, the dualistic religion of ancient Persia, the sheer polytheisms of the ancient Greeks, Romans and Teutons—the mythological religion of the ancient Japanese not being an exception.

The Shintō Pantheon of the ancient Japanese mentioned in the *Kojiki* and the *Nihongi* thoroughly reveals this aspect. The Divine Couple Izanagi and Izanami gave birth to Amaterasu-Ōmikami the female sun, Hiruko the male sun (not so well developed as the Sun-Goddess), Tsukuyomi-no-Mikoto the Moon-God, and Susano-o-no-Mikoto the God of the destructive force of the rainstorm ; and the Sun-Goddess, the Moon-God and the God of the Rainstorm (quite distinct from the Wind-God Shinatsuhiko-no-Kami) each governs one-third of the universe, *i. e.*, the sky, the sea and the realm of night respectively, thus forming a Japanese triad like that of the Homeric Pantheon composed of Zeus the Sky-God, Poseidon the God of the Sea, and Hades (or Pluto) the God of the Under-world. As I have already mentioned, Ame-no-Minaka-nushi-no-Kami the Divine Lord of the Very Centre of Heaven, Takamimusubi-no-Kami[1] the High August Producer, and Kamumimusubi-no-Kami the Divine August Producer, constitute another Japanese triad, along with the triad of Uwazutsu-no-o, Nakazutsu-no-o and Sokozutsu-no-o, these last three divinities in later times known as the Sea-God of Suminoe (the present Sumiyoshi in Settsu Province) or the Divine Protector of sea-faring people, particularly at the time of the Empress Jingō, when she was at war with Korea.

Tagorihime, Tagitsuhime and Ichikishimahime, the three divine daughters of Susano-o-no-Kami, in later times known as the Three Deities of Munakata in Tsukushi, may also be called a Shintō triad.

In the *Nihongi* Kuni-Tokotachi-no-Mikoto or the

[1] We have some other Musubi-no-Kami or Divine Producers, *e. g.*, Tamatsumemusubi, the Soul-detaining Producer, Ikumusubi, the Vivifying Producer, Tarumusubi, the Producer of Perfect Bodily Health and Strength. *Vide E. T. Kg.*, p. 34.

Earthly Eternal Divine Being takes the primacy in the ancient Japanese Pantheon instead of Ame-no-Minakanushi-no-Kami of the *Kojiki* and the *Shinsen-Kisōki*.

Yagokoro-Omoikane-no-Kami, the God of Wisdom, nearly always stands in assisting attendance on Ama-terasu-Ōmikami in issuing the Divine Edicts, just as the Greek Moira, Power of Fate, restricts the supreme power of Zeus, standing beside him, and the Egyptian Goddess Maat performs the same function with the Sun-God Ra.

Moreover, Tachikara-o-no-Kami, the God of Physical Strength, kept the Sun-Goddess outside the Heavenly Rock-Cave and prevented her from re-entering it.

The Sun-Goddess has five sons (Ame-no-Oshiho-mimi-no-Mikoto, Ame-no-Hohi-no-Mikoto, Amatsu-Hikone-no-Mikoto, Ikutsu-Hikone-no-Mikoto, Kuma-nukusubi-no-Mikoto) and a daughter or sister Waka-hirume-no-Mikoto (according to the *Shaku-Nihongi* and *Kujiki* traditions[1]), while the Storm-God Susano-o has three divine daughters mentioned above, along with an-other daughter Suserihime and a son Itakeru-no-Kami.

Among semi-divine personages or culture heroes, ἥρωες in Greek, we have Ōkuninushi-no-Kami, the culture hero and tutelary god of Izumo Province, Sukunahikona-no-Kami, the divine collaborator with

[1] *K. T.*, Vol. VII, p. 606, p. 202.

Ōkuninushi-no-Kami for the advancement of general culture, such as, for example, the reclamation of waste land, clearing the mountains and the rivers of wild beasts, the invention of medicine, incantation, etc., Kotoshironushi-no-Kami, son of Ōkuninushi-no-Kami, Takeminakata-no-Kami, the God of the well-known Suwa Shrine in Shinano Province; as well as Ame-no-Koyane-no-Mikoto and Futotama-no-Mikoto, entrusted, on equal terms, with divine service in the Divine Age, hand in hand with the divine priestess Ame-no-Uzume-no-Mikoto whose divine companion Sarutahiko is another genial apparition as guide to the Heavenly Grandson Ninigi-no-Mikoto on his descent from Heaven to earth.

The ancient War-Gods Takemikazuchi-no-Kami and Futsunushi-no-Kami are very active in the scenes of the heavenly drama and rendered distinguished services to the Imperial House as Messengers to Izumo to persuade Ōkuninushi-no-Kami to surrender his rule over the country to the Heavenly Sovereign.

The part played by the Heavenly Grandson Ninigi-no-Mikoto and his consort Konohana-no-Sakuyahime, a daughter of the Mountain-God Ōyamatsumi-no-Kami and a beautiful maiden goddess like cherry flowers in full bloom, attracts our special attention. It brings us to another dramatic scene of Hikohohodemi-no-Mikoto's visit to the "Royal Dragon Palace" of Ōwatatsumi-no-Kami, the Sea-God, and reveals to us the fascinating episode of his marriage with the daughter of the Sea-God, Toyotamahime by name, during his three years' sojourn there. Ōgetsuhime-no-Kami, otherwise called Toyoukehime-no-Kami, or Uka-no-Mitama, is a Goddess of Food, and during the reign of the Emperor Yūryaku a shrine was erected to her—the present Gekū or Outer Shrine of Ise.

Previous to Izanami's being killed by the Fire-God Kagutsuchi and her descent thereupon to Hades, of which she became the Great Goddess, there had been a Deity of the Underworld, according to the *Kojiki* tradition. Moreover, there are the Deities of good and evil, chiefly in the physical sense of the terms—Kannaobi-no-Kami and Magatsubi-no-Kami respectively.

In studying Japanese mythology, needless to say, the legend of Susano-o-no-Kami and Kushinadahime reminds us of the Greek legend of Perseus and Andromeda, and the characters of Ōkuninushi-no-Kami and Suserihime have a close resemblance to those of the Greek hero Theseus and his wife Ariadne, or Jason and the sorceress Medea, while Izanagi's descent to the Yomi-no-Kuni or Underworld in search of his beloved lost wife Izanami and his inability to regain her for the reason that he broke a promise made with her in Hades have a parallelism in the story of the Greek mythical poet Orpheus and his lamented wife Eurydike.

As the abode of the Homeric deities is on Mt. Olympos, the chief Shintō deities live as a rule in the Plain of High Heaven. At this point the idea of the ancient Japanese is entirely different, as mentioned in Chapter IV, from the belief of the ancient Chinese, who worshipped Heaven itself as a God—Shangti,[1] the Supreme Ruler.

As we have seen above, Shintō is an unequivocal polytheism in the fullest sense of the term. So we have the expressions, "Eighty Myriads of Deities" or "Eight Hundred Myriads of Deities," meaning a great number of deities, in the *Kojiki*, the *Nihongi* and the *Norito* or *Shintō Rituals*, and moreover, in the *Azuma-kagami* (Vol. XXI), an authentic history of Japan, compiled in the 13th century (the Kamakura Period), the number of the deities prayed to on the frequent occasions of disastrous earthquake in the ninth month in the year 1215 (the 3rd year of Kempō) are estimated at 36,000. In certain historical books such deities [3]number more than 1,370,[2] sometimes more than 1,400.

In the *Kishōmon* or *Documentary Oath,* various deities, either Shintoistic or Buddhistic, or sometimes

1   *E.T. Kg.,* pp. 10, 11.

2   *Vide* the *Shimmyōchō* or *Registry of Shintō Shrines (Catalogue of the Names of Shintō Shrines),* recited at the Tōdaiji, a Buddhist temple in Nara.

3   This number is found in a fragment of the *Registries of Shintō Shrines.*

Taoistic, are invoked, and here again we are met with polytheistic Shintō.

In the *Shimmyōchō* or *Registry of Shintō Shrines in the Engishiki* in the 10th century, we have also the names of 2,861 shrines mentioned.

In the 11th century it was settled by order that Imperial Envoys should be sent to special Shintō shrines in Kyōto, in the Home Provinces and in Ise to present annual offerings to the deities therein. The shrines, 22 in number, are as follows :—

(I) SEVEN UPPER SHRINES

    1. The Ise Shrine

    2. The Iwashimizu Shrine

    3. The Kamo Shrine

    4. The Matsunō Shrine

    5. The Hirano Shrine

    6. The Inari Shrine

    7. The Kasuga Shrine

(II) SEVEN MIDDLE SHRINES

    8. The Ōharano Shrine

    9. The Ōmiwa Shrine

  10. The Isonokami Shrine

  11. The Yamato Shrine

  12. The Hirose Shrine

  13. The Tatsuta Shrine

  14. The Sumiyoshi (Suminoe) Shrine

(III) EIGHT LOWER SHRINES

    15. The Hie(i) Shrine
    16. The Umenomiya Shrine
    17. The Yoshida Shrine
    18. The Hirota Shrine
    19. The Gion Shrine
    20. The Kitano Shrine
    21. The Nifu Shrine
    22. The Kibune Shrine

In connection with this let us add that as each shrine mentioned above has as a rule some subordinate shrines attached to it, the whole number of the gods enshrined there is more than double the number of the shrines detailed. Even here the polytheistic aspect of Shintō pretty well reveals itself.

In the course of development of the Shintō religion, much influenced by Buddhism, we find the "Thirty Guardian Deities," as they are called, each of whom is on guard duty, on an allotted day each month throughout the whole year, according to the lunar calendar, either to protect the Imperial Palace from powers of evil or to preserve the Buddha's precious law or Myōhōrengekyō[1] (Skt. *Saddharmapuṇḍarīka-Sūtra*) free from evil influences of hostile demons.

According to the *Jingishōjū*, the Thirty Guardian

---

[1] Otherwise pronounced "Hokkekyō" or "Hokekyō." *Vide* Nanjiō's *Catalogue*, No. 134.

Deities have a special day on which each is on court guardian duty, and the deities and the days mentioned therein are as follows :—

1st Day,	The Deities of Ise
2nd Day,	The God Hachiman
3rd Day,	The Deities of Kamo
4th Day,	The Deity of Matsunō
5th Day,	The Deities of Ōharano
6th Day,	The Deities of Kasuga
7th Day,	The Deities of Hirano
8th Day,	The Deity of the Major Mt. Hie(i)
9th Day,	The Deity of the Minor Mt. Hie(i)
10th Day,	The God Shōshinshi
11th Day,	The Goddess Marōdo
12th Day,	The Divine Hachiōji
13th Day,	The Deity Inari
14th Day,	The Deities of Sumiyoshi (Suminoe)
15th Day,	The Deities of Gion
16th Day,	The Deity of Shakusan
17th Day,	The Deity of Takebe
18th Day,	The Deity of Miyama[1]
19th Day,	The Deity of Hyōzu
20th Day,	The Deity of Nawaka
21st Day,	The Deity of Kibi
22nd Day,	The Deity of Seta

[1] It seems to me that the word "Miyama" is a misprint for "Mikami."

23rd Day,   The Deity of Suwa
24th Day,   The Deity of Hirota
25th Day,   The Deity of Kehi
26th Day,   The Deity of Keta
27th Day,   The Deity of Kashima
28th Day,   The Deity of Kitano
29th Day,   The Deity of Ebumi
30th Day,   The Deity of Kibune
(*Z. G. R. k.*, Vol. III, pp. 61–66).[1]

As I have already mentioned, Shintō, like the Greek and the Roman religions, is a downright polytheism in contradistinction to the monotheism of the Christian religion or Islam, so some of the Shintō believers of older style will side with the New Zealand chief, whose avowed faith is a tribal polytheism, against the intolerant monotheistic religion of Christianity and will defend his own time-honoured traditional faith of polytheism.

Heu-heu, that chief, is reported to have said sarcastically to a Christian missionary :—

"Is there one maker of all things amongst you Europeans ? Is not one a carpenter, another a blacksmith, another a shipbuilder and another a housebuilder ? And so it was in the beginning ; one made

---

1 *Cf.* Nitchō (*d.* 1510), *Hokke-Shintō-Hiketsu.* Kurokawa-Harumura, *Shimmyōchō-Kōshō-Dodaifukō. Vide* Ban-Nobutomo, *Collected Works*, Vol. I, pp. 662–670.

this, another that : Tane made trees, Ru mountains, Tangaroa fish, and so forth. Your religion is of today, ours from remote antiquity. Do not think then to destroy our ancient faith with your fresh-born religion" (Stratton, *Psychology of the Religious Life*, p. 259).

Lucien Lévy-Bruhl also says of the pre-logical mind of nature peoples :—

" ' Every plant', according to him (a chief of the Wallis Islands), 'had its own special creator, who had no power over the other plants'. Primitive mentality is, above all, inclined to the concrete, and has little that is conceptual about it. Nothing astonishes it more than the idea of one universal God" (Lévy-Bruhl, *Primitive Mentality*, p. 321).

CHAPTER VIII

THEANTHROPIC ASPECT OF SHINTŌ DEITIES —SHINTŌ AS A THEANTHROPIC OR HOMOCENTRIC RELIGION

"We see God in man and nature" is an expression of theanthropic religion in contrast with the expression "To see God above man and nature," which is the formula of theocratic religion. In the case of the former, God makes a descent to man and man becomes a God, while the latter draws a sharp demarkation line between God and man—they are *toto cælo* different. The religion of the former centres in man while that of the latter concentrates itself on God. Therefore, theanthropic religion may be termed homocentric and theocratic religion deocentric. According to the former man is anything and everything; according to the latter God is all in all, man is nothing. Now it seems to me Shintō reveals in essence the aspect of theanthropic religion from the beginning.

The theanthropic tendency of Shintō, first of all, betrays itself in anthropolatry or the worship of a divine personage, either during his lifetime or after his death. Hence, we have worship of the Emperor or of a hero, while living or after death; we have

ancestor worship, *i. e.*, the worship of the spirit of the
dead ancestor, and necrolatry, *i. e.*, the worship of the
spirit of the dead, as we have seen above.

The Emperor Ōjin is worshipped as the War-God,
Hachiman by name, although we can trace Buddhist
influence in him ; Sugawara-no-Michizane, an ill-fated
minister, was canonized, so to speak, as a patron god
of culture and calligraphy long after his death. Katō-
Kiyomasa (*d.* 1611), a famous warrior, under Toyotomi-
Hideyoshi, was also canonized as a god by the name
of Seishōkō in close connection with the Buddhist
Nichiren Sect, and at Kumamoto in Kyūshū his tomb
has developed into a shrine and become a centre of
elaborate religious cult and pilgrimage.

Second, anthropomorphism, in the fullest sense of
the term, makes its appearance in Shintō, past and
present.

For instance, the Divine Couple Izanagi and Izanami are completely human, as they appear in the
Kojiki and *Nihongi* myths. The Sun-Goddess Amaterasu-Ōmikami is also quite anthropomorphic in a
dramatic scene in front of the Heavenly Rock-Cave,
or when she came into conflict with her impetuous
brother Susano-o-no-Kami. And we are told, according to one of the *Kojiki* and *Nihongi* myths, that
Hitokotonushi-no-Kami, a God Incarnate, "Arahitogami," in archaic Japanese, spent a day side by side

with the Emperor Yūryaku, another God manifest in man, on horseback, hunting wild animals in Mt. Katsuragi (*E. T. K.*, p. 319; *E. T. N.*, Vol. I, p. 341).

Third, the Shintō deities, so far as they partake of the nature of theanthropic religion, have human limitations in their characters and actions. Even the Divine Couple Izanagi and Izanami, did not know how to act in coition, when they entered into conjugal relations, until the wagtail suggested it to them. Curiously enough in this case the bird is a teacher of the deities.

Izanagi and Izanami gave birth to an imperfect child, for instance, Hiruko, the leech child, was born to them, which at the age of three could not walk by itself. The child is imperfect, because the parents are not perfect, never omnipotent. The hidden cause of the birth of an imperfect child is incomprehensible even to the Divine Parents, so they inquired of the Heavenly Deities about the matter (*E. T. K.*, p. 21. *E. T. N.*, Vol. I, p. 15), and the latter resorted to the means of grand divination and ascertained the true cause.

According to the *Kogoshūi*, when Ōtokonushi-no-Kami, the God of Land, saw that the rice plants in his fields began prematurely to die, he was greatly dismayed and listened to the warning of certain diviners. The fact that even the divine beings so often resorted to divination proclaims that they are not omnipotent. So far as they are not omnipotent, they must die. Izanami, for instance, was burnt to death when she was delivered of fire or the God of Fire, Kagutsuchi by name (*E. T. N.*, Vol. I, p. 21). Amewakahiko, the heavenly messenger to Izumo, Ukemochi-no-Kami, the Goddess of Food, and Waka-hirume-no-Mikoto, the Morning or Spring Sun-God-dess, died, being killed by their opponents (*E. T. N.*, Vol. I, p. 45), just as Sarpedon, the divine son of Zeus, was killed on the battlefield, and Ares, the Greek God of War, was mortally wounded by the hero Diomedes and bellowed like an army 10,000 strong, according to Homer (*Iliad*, , 971–992). Even the Great Sun-Goddess was wounded by her shuttle when she was alarmed and about to retire into the Rock-Cave, because her brother exceedingly rude in conduct made violence to her; and she was enticed to come out of the Rock-Cave again, being allured by the pleasing words and the bright mirror—a symbol of the sun's disc—shown to her. By herself she felt lonesome at the Ise Shrine, so she disclosed her divine will in a dream to the Emperor Yūryaku to invite Toyouke-no-Ōkami, the Food-Goddess, from Tamba to Ise, to wait upon her and serve food, morning and evening, as the ladies in waiting do to the Emperor at court (*Toyouke-no-Miya-Gishikichō.*

G. R. k., Vol. I, p. 53. *Cf. Jingū-Zōreishū. G. R. k.*, Vol. I, p. 160).

All these incidents show that Shintō deities somehow or other have human limitations and *ipso facto* the Shintō religion proves to be a theanthropic religion.

Shintō considers all natural phenomena as analogous with occurrences in human society, so in Shintō the idea of creation is absent but procreation or begetting is the key-note in explaining nature. Therefore we read in the *Nihongi*, for example, "They (Izanagi and Izanami) next produced the sea, then the rivers and then the mountains" (*E. T. N.*, Vol. I, p. 18). Unlike the Hebrew Yahweh, the Divine Couple Izanagi and Izanami never created the universe from nothing, as the Biblical creation story, which is theocratic in essence, tells us of the relation of Yahweh and the universe, but begat the seas, rivers, mountains, the Great-Eight-Island-Country, even trees and herbs, just as a man and a woman beget children in marriage. Therefore later on Shintō showed a tendency to develop itself into pantheism or pantheistic naturalism, because God and nature are not quite different in essence, but natural objects such as mountains, rivers, trees, and herbs—men not excepted—all are born of the Divine Couple Izanagi and Izanami, *i. e.*, they are all offspring of Divinity. They are *ipso facto* themselves divine. In Shintoistic belief, "Not miracles but natural law" is the dominating power to which nature and man are alike subject. Therefore, when Konohana-no-Sakuya-hime, the beautiful maiden and favorite consort of the Heavenly Grandson Ninigi-no-Mikoto, became pregnant in the course of a single night, he suspected that it could not be his own child, because he thought that even the August Grandson of the Heavenly Deities must be unable to cause pregnancy in so short a time; such being un-common, extraordinary, i. e., in violation of the ordinary law of Nature (E. T. N., Vol. I, p. 88).

We are very familiar with the descriptions of Yahweh's miracles in the Old Testament. Yahweh stands high above natural law. This is one of the characteristics of theocratic religion. On the contrary, in Shintō, Gods alike with men are subject to natural law and cannot escape from it. This is an aspect of theanthropic religion. In theocratic religion God stands high above man and nature, while in theanthropic religion God is in nature and man, and divinity is inherent in humanity and nature. In theanthropic religion man and nature are placed on the same footing as God; "The Gods are immortal men, men are mortal Gods," as Herakleitos characterizes it. Thus, in theanthropic religion the relation of God and man is quite reciprocal; and so, "Do ut des" occurs be-tween God and man. Therefore, according to Livy, once in a crisis an ancient Roman general addressed himself to his Goddess of War, praying to her :—

"Bellona, if thou wilt today grant us victory, then I promise thee a temple" (Clifford H. Moore, *Religious Thought of the Greeks*, p. 228).

In like manner, in Homeric Greece Apollon was invoked :—

"Hear me, God of the silver bow! whose care
Chrysa surrounds, and Cilla's lovely vale;
Whose sov'reign sway o'er Tenedos extends;
O Smintheus, hear! if e'er my offer'd gifts
Found favour in thy sight; if e'er to thee
I burn'd the fat of bulls and choicest goats,
Grant me this boon—upon the Grecian host
Let thine unerring darts avenge my tears"

(Iliad, I, 45—52).

The case is the same with the theanthropic religion of Shintō. For instance, when the Empress Jingō prayed to the deities for victory over Korea, the deities revealed their divine will thus :— " If you present us with a ship and rice fields for an offering, or rather a bribe, literally speaking, we will bestow a rich country upon you " (*Cf. E. T. N.*, Vol. I, p. 233). Δῶρα πείθειν καὶ θεοὺς λόγος (*Medea*, 964), as Euripides puts it. This is just the praying formula, " Do ut des." To cite another instance, when the Emperor Ingyō got no game a-hunting all day long in the Island of Awaji, divination revealed that it was by the divine will of Izanagi that game in the island was unobtainable; and the same God disclosed his will, saying :—" If you obtain a beautiful pearl from the bottom of the Sea of Akashi and send it to me as an offering, I shall in return let you have much game" (*Cf. E. T. N.*, Vol. I, pp. 322, 323).

In the *Jōei-Shikimoku* or *Administrative Code of the Jōei Era*,[1] we read :— "Devotional reverence on the part of man makes a Deity more and more supreme, while by virtue of the Divine Grace man's life is doubly blessed" (*G. R. k.*, Vol. XIV, p. 1).

This formula shows that God and man are always in reciprocal relations, and necessarily they depend upon each other. In short, it is nothing but another way of expressing the religious formula "Do ut des."[2]

---

[1] The Jōei Era falls in 1232.

[2] In Sanskrit we have the expression *Dehime dadāmi te*, and in Greek a similar idea is given in the expression, 'Εγώ εἰμι σὺ καὶ ʼσὺ ἐγώ.

CHAPTER IX

SHINTŌ IS THE JAPANESE NATIONAL RELIGION OF NATURAL GROWTH

Like the religion of ancient Greece, that of ancient Rome, or that of Israel, Shintō is indigenous to its own soil, and it is in its origin a mental production of the Japanese people as a whole, so it thus had no particular founder, as had Buddhism, Christianity, or Islam. Shintō is as old as the Japanese nation herself and will have its existence as long as the nation endures. The religion of ancient Greece died out, as the Greek nation perished, the religion of ancient Rome is no more, the Roman people having ceased to be. The case is the same with the ancient religions of Egypt, Babylonia, Assyria, etc. The Japanese nation, however, has never ceased, so her own religion maintains itself. Wherever the nation is, there also is her own religion. In short, Shintō is the national religion of the Japanese people and had no individual founder, as was the case with any other national religion.

As I have already mentioned, Amaterasu-Ōmikami has an aspect of not only the solar deity but of the human ancestral deity, as an ancient divine progenitress of the Imperial family. So the Sun-Goddess Amaterasu-Ōmikami is, first in origin, the tutelary Ancestral Goddess of the Imperial family, and then, that of the Japanese people at large. By degrees, the solar aspect of Amaterasu-Ōmikami almost passing into oblivion, her ancestral character has become predominant. So, the Japanese people today worship Amaterasu-Ōmikami at the Ise Shrine as their national Ancestral Deity as well as the Great Ancestress of the Imperial family.

As Amaterasu-Ōmikami is the tutelary Ancestral Deity, the Emperor Jimmu oftentimes invoked the Goddess to help his Imperial army during his campaigns in the Yamato district. On the part of the Goddess, she sometimes disclosed her divine will in the same Emperor's dreams or sometimes revealed omens by sending him a divine messenger crow or by presenting a divine sword, always giving unseen protection from Heaven. In the course of the Empress Jingō's conquest of Korea, the *aramitama* or rough spirit of Amaterasu-Ōmikami called "Tsukisakaki-Izunomitama-Amazakaru-Mukatsuhime-no-Mikoto" made its appearance and brought Providential assistance to the Empress. In the Mongol invasion in the 13th century, a gale of divine wind sent from the Ise Shrine overtook the enemy's fleet off the coast of Kyūshū and scattered it, the result being destruction of nearly all the hostile ships. This is, according to the people's faith, because the National Guardian Goddess Amaterasu-Ōmikami in response to the earnest prayer of the Ex-Emperor Kameyama for divine help sent a cataclysm upon the invading enemy. Tradition has it that out of tens of thousands of Mongol warriors only three men escaped the peril of the deep. Therefore, in the *Jinnō-Shōtōki* by Kitabatake-Chikafusa, it runs as follows :—" A great number of the Mongol warships came across the sea to attack Japan. In naval battles that were fought on the Tsukushi coasts, deities themselves appeared and participated in the country's behalf. All of a sudden, a gale of wind sprang up and speedily destroyed the numberless vessels of the invaders. Indeed, it was a Providential help from High, even at so remote a time from the Divine Age ! A clear evidence of the Providence that never failed to save our country at a national crisis !" (Vol. V, 24).

Fujiwara-no-Tameuji, the Imperial Envoy, sent to the Ise Shrine, to invoke the Ancestral Guardian Goddess there, overwhelmed with gratitude to the national Deity for the deliverance, composed a thirty-one syllable poem which is here rendered as follows:—

"Responsive to my fervent prayer for Heaven's Elect,
   In wrath divine our Goddess with her winds hath swept
The seas, where-o'er the foe a mighty fleet had sent,
And to destruction are his warships dashed and rent."

Ōnakatomi-no-Sukeharu (*d.* 1324), a Shintō priest

attached to the Kasuga-Wakamiya Shrine also says :—

"O ! Waves tempestuous from the Western Main !

Deem not but that your rage is spent in vain,

Against these sacred Isles of Yamato,

Where Heaven's protection doth unceasing reign !"
The author of a Japanese history entitled *Masukagami*
remarks on this extraordinary occurrence thus :—
"Consequently, we realize that our country is still
under the supernatural protection of the divinities"
(*N. B. Z. h.,* Vol. XXIV, p. 213).

A similar interposition is observed in the case of
the Assyrian King Sennacherib's invasion (701 B. C.)
of Israel, when the Assyrian soldiers were seized with
bubonic plague cursefully sent upon their camp by the
wrathful Yahweh, the national warder of Israel, and
185,000 men were killed in a night (*II Kings*, XIX,
32–37). "As birds flying, so will the Lord of hosts
defend Jerusalem ; then shall the Assyrian fall with the
sword" (*Isa.,* XXXI, 5, 8).

As the ancient Athenians, grateful to the winds
that assisted the Greek fleet at Artemision, instituted
a cult of Boreas, the Wind-God of the ancient Greeks
(Farnell, *Outline History of Greek Religion,* p. 97), so,
likewise, the ruler of Japan, deeply thankful to the
Wind-Deity at Ise, who granted his prayer and aided
him in his successful resistance to the Mongol invasion,
raised the rank of the Shrine of the Wind-Deity at

Ise and honoured it with official offerings, while the Authorities concerned paid homage to both the Outer and the Inner Shrine of Ise (Watarai-Ieyuki, *Ruiju-Jingihongen, Z. Z. G. R. k.*, Vol. I, p. 60).

Not only the Goddess of the Ise Shrine but the War-God Hachiman, Takeminakata the God of the Suwa Shrine, Ōyamatsumi the God of the Mishima Shrine of Iyo Province and even the Gods of Suminoe (originally the three guardian deities of navigators, and divine guides and protectors of the Empress Jingō on her expedition to Korea) were all divine warders and protectors of the Japanese people against foreign enemies. Particularly, Hachiman, the God of War, was invoked, when the Mongol fleet came to assail us. The Ex-Emperor Kameyama sent an Imperial Envoy to Otokoyama in the suburb of Kyōto to pray to the War-God Hachiman there for aid in repulsing the foreign invaders. Even today we can see the great tablet set up high at the entrance to the Shrine of Hachiman at Hakozaki in Kyūshū, and on one side of that tablet we read :—

"Foreign Invaders ! Be Vanquished !"

Tradition has it that the inscription on the tablet is an autograph of the Emperor Daigo.[1]

Even Hitokotonushi-no-Kami, the God of Mt.

---

1 Some ascribe the inscription to the Ex-Emperor Kameyama, while others suggest it may be by the Emperor Gotsuchimikado.

Katsuragi, uttered his oracle through a courtier :— "I am a guardian spirit against traitors and foreign invaders" (*Genkōshakusho*, Vol. XV. *K. T.*, Vol. XIV, p. 884).

With the ancient Greeks the Japanese themselves said of their victory: "Not we, but our national deities have carried the day." [1]

Although Shintō is very tolerant, compared with other national religions, yet in a way it has a jealous deity, like the Israelite Yahweh or the Assyrian national God Assur. Therefore, when Buddhism was first introduced into this country, a controversy arose as to whether the foreign deities were to be accepted, and if so, would the national deities become angry. Hence the foreign deities *versus* the national deities !

Even long after the Buddhist religion was admitted, the highest national Goddess Amaterasu-Ōmikami refused to have a Buddhist temple built near the Ise Shrine and, in the reign of the Emperor Kōnin, sent a curse (*Shoku-Nihongi*, XXXVI. *K. T.*, Vol. II, p. 637).

So, the Imperial Guardian Priestesses of the Ise and the Kamo Shrines were not allowed to speak of Buddhas or Buddhist Sūtras and people were ordered to avoid the use of Buddhist terminology in the holy precincts of the Ise Shrine. For instance, utterance at the Ise Shrine was strictly forbidden of the follow-

1 *Cf.* Martin P. Nilsson, *History of Greek Religion*, p. 234.

ing "Buddhistic Terms" :—Buddhas, sūtras, stūpas, monks, upāsakas (Buddhist lay believers), Buddhist temples, Buddhist holy meals, death, graves, etc. (*Kōtaijingū-Gishikichō. G. R. k.*, Vol. I, p. 4. *Engishiki*, Vol. V. *K. T.*, Vol. XIII, p. 189).

The practice of the worship of the Polar Star God, who was then very popular in Japan, was prohibited by order during the 9th month in the year 811, because the Imperial Guardian Priestess was, in that month, to proceed to the Ise Shrine from Kyōto and the Polar Star God, being of Chinese Taoistic origin, was objectionable. Here we find the national Shintō Goddess Amaterasu-Ōmikami *versus* a foreign star god (*Nihon-Isshi*, Vol. XIX. *K. T.*, Vol. VI, p. 201).

The same exclusiveness of nationalistic Shintō against its rival religion Buddhism was displayed in the resentment of the Imperial Buddhist monk Gyō-nyo (*Zasu-Nikki* or *Imperial Buddhist Abbot's Diary*), when the Emperor Higashiyama solemnized the Shintō Enthronement Ceremony in 1687 (the 4th year of Jōkyō).

Every national deity is bound to its own land or soil. So, for example, the Syrian captain Naaman, in order to worship Yahweh in Syria, was obliged to take "two mules' burden of earth" of the Jordan into his country (*II Kings*, v, 17). A Shintō deity and the land of Japan are inseparably connected, so that the Kusanagi Sword, the Divine Emblem of the Atsuta

Shrine, could not be taken away out of the land of Japan, even though a Buddhist monk Dōgyō of Shiragi (Silla) in 668 (during the reign of the Emperor Tenchi) sacrilegiously attempted to make off with it to his own land of Korea, because a heaven-sent tempest on the sea prevented his ship from sailing; that is to say, the Kusanagi Sword would not separate itself from its native soil of Japan (*E. T. N.*, Vol. II, p. 290. *E. T. Kg.*, note 118, pp. 84, 85).

CHAPTER X

ANCIENT SHINTŌ PRACTICES

I CULTS OR RITES

Anciently as was the Shintō religion inseparably connected with agriculture, the Niinaematsuri[1] (Shinjō-sai) or Autumnal Harvest Festival or Feast of New Rice Crops in Autumn was from the oldest times one of the most important festivals in Shintō. We can trace the origin of the festival to the so-called Divine Age, when, tradition says, the Japanese people lived in the Plain of High Heaven. At that time Amaterasu-Ōmikami herself conducted the Feast of New Rice Crops in Heaven (*E. T. N.*, Vol. I, p. 40), and Ame-wakahiko, the heavenly messenger and traitor, is reported to have observed the same feast (*E. T. N.*, Vol. I, p. 66). And also in ancient Japan it may have been quite customary to observe the Feast of New Rice Crops in every family household, however high or low in social position.

The *Hitachifudoki* or *Ancient Topography of Hitachi Province* thus records :—" Old people say that once upon a time when going round the country the

[1] Sometimes pronounced " Niinamematsuri."

Ancestral Deity asked, as darkness set in, a night's shelter for himself of the Deity of Mt. Fuji. This the Deity refused, because on that evening the Harvest Festival or Feast of New Millet Crop was being solemnized and his abode was therefore taboo. The religious law of abstinence is too strict to admit a sacrilegious stranger " (Kurita, *Hyōchū-Kofudoki*, p. 5).

In the Harvest Festival the new rice obtained in that year is offered up to the family or clannish deities and at the same time it is served to all the kinsfolk. Therefore it is a communal feast between deities and men—a holy communion, so to say, among a religious community in old Japan. In the Bear-Festival of the Ainu, the feast is a holy communion in rude form in a stage of nature religion, because deities and men alike are in common feasted with and partake of the same flesh of the sacred totem animal, the bear.

This communal feast of the Japanese is otherwise called "Naorai" or the "After-Feast." Later on in the autumn of the year in which a new Emperor succeeded to the Throne the same festival was observed on a larger scale than usual, being called the Ōnie-matsuri (Daijōsai) or Great Harvest Festival, and it constituted an integral part of the Coronation Ceremony of the Emperor. According to the *Jingiryō* or *Shintō Administrative Law*, as a prelude to the Great Harvest Festival, the Emperor, as a Pontifex Maximus, observed two forms of abstinence ; one most strict (called "Ma-imi" or "Principal Abstinence," through the period of which a person devotes himself to the religious performances only), the other not so strict (called "Araimi" or "Preliminary Abstinence"). The former lasts for three days and the latter for a month (*Ryō-no-Gige.* K. T., vol. XII, p. 71).

The historical origin of the Ōniematsuri, discriminated from the Niinaematsuri, dates back to the year 673 in the reign of the Emperor Temmu (5th day, 12th month, 2nd year. *E. T. N.,* vol. II, p. 324).

The reader will thus see that the Feast of New Rice Crops is a festival of thanksgiving to the tutelary deities, at the end of the year, for the abundance of new rice crops, and, this being so, it is quite natural that people have in advance at the beginning of the year, as husbandmen commence their spring work in the paddy fields, a festival of prayer to the deities for bountiful autumnal crops. This spring festival is called the Toshigoimatsuri or Kinensai mentioned in the *Engishiki* (901–923).

In the Imperial Court was observed, during summer and winter of each year, the Ōharai or Rite of the Great Purification, the details of which need not be given here since Western readers are doubtless familiar with them through Prof. Florenz's English translation of the *Ritual of the Great Purification.* We

have many other minor annual rites of Shintō mentioned
in the *Engishiki*, which limits of time and space forbid
my enlarging upon here.

In the remote age of the deities, we are informed
that there were already some sorts of religious rites,
because the *Nihongi* tells us that Takamimusubi-no-
Mikoto in Heaven worshipped the deities with due
Shintō ceremony on behalf of the Heavenly Grandson,
setting up sacred trees and stones (*E. T. N.*, Vol. I
pp. 81, 82), and that the Emperor Jimmu worshipfully
conducted the rite of adoring the Heavenly Ancestral
Deities in the holy precincts in the Tomi Mountains
(*ibid.*, Vol. I, p. 134).

In the reign of the Emperor Sujin a religious rite
of the same character was held at Kasanui Village in
Yamato Province, in honour of the Divine Mirror and
Sword, according to the *Kogoshūi* (pp. 36, 37). The
God-fearing Emperor ordered the removal, with special
respect and care, of those two Divine Emblems from
the Imperial Court to the new shrine erected for them
at Kasanui, and the same evening all the courtiers who
performed the rite of the removal were present, singing
a divine anthem and enjoying a communal feast all
night long.

According to the *Kujiki*, Umashimade-no-Mikoto
prayed for the longevity of the Emperor and tranquil-
lized the souls of the Emperor and Empress by virtue of

the "Ten Sacred Auspicious Treasures,"—the Mirror of the Offing, the Mirror of the Shore, the Eight-hand-span Sword, the Life-inspiring Jewel, the Jewel of Perfect Health and Strength, the Jewel of Resuscitating the Dead, the Jewel Warding Evil from Roads, the Serpent-preventing Scarf, the Bee-preventing Scarf, and the Scarf of Various Materials and Efficacies (*Tennō-Hongi. K. T.*, Vol. VII, pp. 264, 321, 322. *Vide* W.G. Aston, *Shintō, the Way of the Gods*, p. 293. Also, *E. T. N.*, Vol. II, p. 373). This is the origin of the Mitamashizume-no-Matsuri (Chinkonsai) or Spirit-quieting Ceremony for the Weal of the Emperor, as mentioned in Chapter IV.

In the reign of the Emperor Temmu the worship of the spirits of the Imperial Ancestors was observed by the Emperor in 681 (*E. T. N.*, Vol. II, p. 351) and in 679 the same Emperor worshipped at the Mausoleum of the Empress Saimyō (*E. T. N.*, Vol. II, p. 341).

The villagers of Arima in Kii Province, where there is the grave of the Goddess Izanami, according to the *Nihongi* tradition, worshipped that divine spirit at her grave-shrine, presenting flowers as an offering (*E. T. N.*, Vol. I, p. 21).

The Inu Shrine in Aika-Gun, Izumo Province, dedicated to Ame-no-Mikatsuhime (*Ancient Topography of Izumo Province*) is an ancient mound with a sacred tree growing on it, which symbolizes the divinity, according to modern archæological investigation.

The case is the same with the Kawai Shrine, which is nothing but another very old mound, traditionally known as the grave of Takekonomikoto-Kawainao, descended from the Mononobe family (*Shimanekenshi*, Vol. III, p. 760).

It is a well-known fact that the grave of the Emperor Ōjin has grown into the Shrine of Konda-Hachiman in Kawachi.

According to the *Engishiki*, the Annual Shintō Festivals are classified into three as follows :—

(I) The Greater Festival :

> The Ōniematsuri (Daijōsai) or Great Harvest Festival at the Ceremony of the Enthronement of the Emperor.

(II) The Middle Festivals :

(1) The Toshigoimatsuri (Kinensai) or Festival for Praying for Rich Harvest.

(2) The Tsukinamimatsuri or Monthly Festivals.

(3) The Kanniematsuri (Kannamematsuri or Jinjōsai) or Imperial Festival at the Ise Shrine on which occasion new rice of the year is presented to the Ancestral Sun-Goddess.

(4) The Niinaematsuri (Niinamematsuri or Shinjōsai) or Autumnal Festival (the Feast of New Rice Crops).

(5) The Festival of the Kamo Shrine.

(III) Lesser Festivals :

(1) The Ōimi-no-Matsuri or Festival of Praying for Abundant Rice Crops at the Hirose Shrine.

(2) The Kazenokami-Matsuri or Festival for Propitiating the Wind-God to Favour a Rich Harvest for the Year.

(3) The Hanashizume-no-Matsuri or Festival of Appeasing the Evil Deities of Epidemic Diseases.

(4) The Saigusa-no-Matsuri or Festival of the Izagawa Shrine in Komori-Machi, Nara, when the *sake*-casks sacred to the Deity were decorated with "saigusa" or wild lily flowers.

(5) The Ainiematsuri (Ainamematsuri) or Feast of New Rice Crops before the Niinaematsuri.

(6) The Mitamashizume-no-Matsuri or Spirit-quieting Ceremony.

(7) The Hishizume-no-Matsuri or Festival of Appeasing the Fire-God.

(8) The Michiaematsuri or Festival of the Road Deities.

(9) The Sono-Karakami-no-Matsuri or Festival of the Sono and Kara Deities worshipped at the Imperial Household Department.

(10) The Festival of the Matsunō Shrine.

(11) The Festival of the Hirano Shrine.

(12)　The Festival of the Kasuga Shrine.

(13)　The Festival of the Ōharano Shrine.

(*Engishiki. K. T.*, Vol. XIII, p. 92).

II OFFERINGS

(1) SACRIFICIAL OFFERINGS

Sacrificial offerings in Shintō usually consist of rice, vegetables, edible sea-weed, *sake*, fishes, birds, animals, etc. At the festival in honour of Mitoshi-no-Kami the Deity of Rice Crops, a white horse, a white wild boar, and a white fowl are sacrificed, according to the *Ritual of Praying for Rich Harvest* and the *Kogoshūi.*

To the Deity of the Nifukawakami Shrine either a white or a black horse is very often offered in order thereby to implore rain or to have long continued rains stopped (*Shoku-Nihongi*, Vol. XXIV and Vol. XXXIV. *K. T.*, Vol. II, pp. 411, 604). I do not know in the present case if such horses are sacrificial offerings in the strict sense of the term, or whether they may be offered to the Deity of the Nifukawakami Shrine for riding purposes.

According to the *Nihongi,* in 642 (the reign of the Empress Kōkyoku), horses and cattle were sacrificed to the deities of various shrines (*E. T. N.*, Vol. II, p. 174).

The *Shoku-Nihongi* tells us that in 791, *i. e.*, in the 10th year of Enryaku, the people in Ise, Owari....and Kii were forbidden to sacrifice oxen to a Chinese deity

(*Shoku-Nihongi*, Vol. XL. *K. T.*, Vol. II, p. 777).

According to the *Nihon-Reiiki*, a certain rich man in the reign of the Emperor Shōmu (701–756) annually, for 7 years, sacrificed an ox to appease a wrathful Chinese deity (Keikai, *Nihon-Reiiki. G. R. k.*, Vol. XVI, p. 53).

Cases of human sacrifice are very often mentioned in Japanese historical books of old, but some of them are quite legendary, and those deities that are so blood-thirsty and cruel in character as to require a human victim seem to be *numen loci*. The legendary maiden Kushinadahime was to be sacrificed to a monster serpent, regarded as an awful deity, on the upper reaches of the River Hi in Izumo (*E. T. N.*, Vol. I, p. 52).

In the reign of the Emperor Nintoku, a certain Kowakubi of Musashi Province was sacrificed to the River-Deity to appease it and induce it not to break the embankments of the river (*E. T. N.*, Vol. I, p. 281).

When Prince Yamatotakeru, on a sea voyage, was overtaken by a violent storm, his consort Tachibana-hime voluntarily sacrificed herself by plunging into the sea in order that the life of the Imperial Prince might be preserved (*E. T. N.*, Vol. I, p. 206).

The "hitobashira" or "human pillar," as it is called, frequent at the building of bridges across rivers, and during river or seashore embankment works, may be considered as a kind of human sacrifice.

To cite an instance here out of many, the case of

the hitobashira of a certain Sekihachi-Yasutaka in the 16th century is to be considered historically genuine. In order to make complete the embankment works of the Asase-Ishikawa River, he sacrificed himself most willingly, thereby appeasing the anger of the River-Deity, and at the same time constituting himself forever the guardian spirit of the river.

According to Jean Crasset, a catholic missionary and an eye-witness of feudal Japan, it was then widely in vogue that some number of samurai or retainers of daimyō or feudal lords killed themselves beneath the foundation stones of the walls of a castle and thus they became of their own free will hitobashira or human pillars—human sacrifices to the demons of the site—and at the same time new guardian spirits of the castle.

Needless to mention here the "junshi"—a wife's self-immolation that she might accompany her husband after death or a retainer's suicide in order to follow his dead lord to another world—of which instances in Japanese history are so numerous. The Emperors Suinin and Kōtoku forbade such barbarous customs (*E. T. N.*, Vol. I, p. 181; Vol. II, p. 220) and the *Ryō-no-Gige* compiled in the year 833 (the 10th year of Ter-hō) tells us that, by Imperial command, similar prohibition was made in Shinano, where they were prevalent.[1]

The Japanese people have the expression "Blood-Feast in honour of the War-God," which means a ceremony of offering human blood shed by killing some of the enemies encountered first on the battlefield or a war captive caught by chance immediately before going to battle.   So, like the Greek War-God Ares, the Japanese War-God may seem to demand a human sacrifice.

In the *Heike-Monogatari* we read :—

"The warrior Hatakeyama hung at his saddle the head of an enemy, whom he had killed on the field of battle, in order to make a first sacrifice of it to the God of War" (*Heike-Monogatari*. *T. A. S. J.*, Vol. XLIX, p. 117).

In my personal opinion, however, it is rather doubtful whether the Japanese War-God was actually worshipped in camps with human sacrifices, as legend goes.   The descriptions in some Japanese books of wars may, I conjecture, have been fabricated to imitate Chinese authors.

What I have mentioned above about human sacrifice, "hitobashira" or human pillars, and "junshi" or self-immolation (or willing self-sacrifice) may be some-

---

1   The Imperial command says :—
  "It is quite customary that in Shinano Province the life of a wife is sacrificed to her husband in death, but such an inhuman custom should be abolished and rectified through ethical education (*Vide ibid.*, Vol. I. *K. T.*, Vol. XII, p. 53).

what mythical or legendary[1], but the cases quoted illustrate the same principle that without such offerings of high value in a great crisis of a state or community the deities cannot be propitiated.

(2) VOTIVE OFFERINGS

As sacred votive gifts different kinds of weapons are offered up to deities, and the custom began in the reign of the Emperor Suinin. Therefore in the *Nihongi* we read :—"The practice of offering weapons in sacrifice to the Gods of Heaven and Earth probably had its origin at this time" (*E. T. N.*, Vol. I, p. 178). Even nowadays the "ema" or tablet with a horse drawn on it, as also swords, are very common offerings at a Shintō shrine.

III DEITIES' DWELLINGS OR SHRINES

The present writer is of opinion that the origin of Shintō shrines is in the main two-fold : one source is in the grove and the other in the grave. The first case is proved from the fact that the Japanese word "mori" meaning grove or forest is, in archaic Japanese, used quite synonymously for the word "jinja" or shrine.

According to the *Nihongi*, in the Divine Age a holy site with sacred trees and stones around was constructed in order to worship deities invoked there.

---

[1] *Cf.* A. Fairbanks, *Handbook of Greek Religion*, p. 105.

These holy sites surrounded with trees were no less than groves, and they served as ancient shrines, as was the case with the ancient Teutons.

According to the *Nihongi*, when Izanami died she was buried in a cave, and was worshipped every year with flower offerings.

This cave is nothing but an ancient tomb, and it at once became considered as a divine abode or shrine, in front of which the worship of the spirit of the dead Izanami was conducted.

In the reigns of the Emperors Jimmu and Sujin there were numbers of both Heavenly and Earthly shrines (*E. T. N.*, Vol. I, pp. 120, 154).

Tradition has it that the Izumo Shrine was erected in the Divine Age to the God Ōkuninushi-no-Kami of Izumo who ceded his country to the Heavenly Grandson (*E. T. N.*, Vol. I, p. 80).

The Ōmiwa Shrine in Yamato is dedicated to the God Ōnamuchi, and its beginning was also in the Divine Age, according to the *Nihongi* tradition (*E. T. N.*, Vol. I, p. 61).

The Ise Shrine of Amaterasu-Ōmikami was in its origin a shrine first founded in Kasanui Village, Yamato Province, in the reign of the Emperor Sujin, according to the *Kogoshūi*, and the emblem of the Sun-Goddess enshrined there was the sacred Eight-hand-span or Large Mirror. The same Mirror, symbolizing Amaterasu-Ōmikami, was transferred to the Ise Shrine, under the guardianship of the Imperial Princess Yamatohime, a Shintō Vestal Virgin whose predecessor was Toyosuki-Irihime, a daughter of the Emperor Sujin.

This Shintō Shrine of Ise has been dedicated to Amaterasu-Ōmikami, and called the Inner Shrine of Ise, in contradistinction to the Outer Shrine of Ise, which was first constructed in the reign of the Emperor Yūryaku and dedicated to the Food-Goddess, Toyouke-Daijin, divine waitress to the Sun-Goddess in the Inner Shrine of Ise.

The renowned Atsuta Shrine was dedicated to the Divine Kusanagi or Herb-quelling Sword in the reign of the Emperor Keikō, although the Divine Sword together with the Divine Mirror was once worshipped in a holy site surrounded with sacred trees and stones at Kasanui Village in Yamato, in the reign of the Emperor Sujin.

Let us remind the reader of the replicas of the original Divine Mirror and Sword, which were made in the reign of the Emperor Sujin, and the Mirror has been preserved at the Imperial Court as divine warder of the Emperor against all powers of evil.

This is the origin of the Kashikodokoro or Imperial Court Shrine otherwise called the Imperial Holy of Holies, or the Imperial Household Sanctum, now maintained in the Imperial Palace of Tōkyō.

The famous Isonokami Shrine was erected in the reign of the Emperor Sujin in honour of the Great God Takefutsu and the Ten Sacred Auspicious Treasures brought from the Plain of High Heaven by Nigihayahino-Mikoto, according to the *Kujiki* tradition (Vol. V. *K. T.*, Vol. VII, p. 271).

Thus the number of shrines in the Empire increased year after year until, according to the *Engishiki*, they were estimated at 2,861; and in the eleventh century, during the reign of the Emperor Shirakawa, 22 shrines out of many were selected to receive special homage from the Imperial Government. The names of these selected shrines, being worthy of mention, are detailed in Chapter VII.

IV PRIESTHOOD

At the very beginning ancient Shintō seems to have had no priestly corporation to speak of, or at any rate no well organized body.

As a rule the paterfamilias of each family is the chief priest. The head of each family is both father and priest. While living, he is called the *ujinokami* or the head of the family and he becomes the *ujigami* or tutelary God of a family after his death. Therefore the *ujinokami* (or family chief) is a living *ujigami* (or family God) while the *ujigami* (or family God) is a dead *ujinokami* (or family chief), so to speak. Thus Amaterasu-Ōmikami, the ancestress of the Japanese

Imperial Family, is at once a sovereign and a priestess, because she herself in the Plain of High Heaven is traditionally reported by the ancient Chronicles as making divine ceremonial robes as a votive gift to the Heavenly Deities. And each local Kokusō or chieftain is also a priest as well as the political governor of a locality. In time of trouble, however, we have a specially inspired personage, whose duty it is to disclose the divine will to the people at large ; as, for example, Ame-no-Uzume played before the Heavenly Rock-Cave the part of an inspired religious dancer to entice the Sun-Goddess to come out from her retreat, when she had concealed herself in the Heavenly Rock-Cave and utter darkness thereupon ensued.

The Empress Jingō and Ikatsu-no-Omi, according to the *Nihongi,* were possessed by the deities, at the time of war with Korea (*E. T. N.,* Vol. I, p. 225). Ōtataneko, in the reign of the Emperor Sujin, and the sibyl Himiko of Tsukushi, are both divinely inspired personages. In the Divine Age Ame-no-Hohi-no-Mikoto and his descendants were attached to the Izumo Shrine as hereditary priests in charge of the worship of Ōkuninushi-no-Kami of Izumo ; and Toyo-suki-Irihime and Nunaki-Irihime were Imperial Guardian Priestesses or Japanese Vestal Virgins sacred, respectively, to Amaterasu-Ōmikami and Ōkunitama-no-Kami of Yamato, each taking charge of one of the two

Shrines, when the Emperor Sujin ordered the removal of the Divine Mirror and Sword from the Imperial Palace in honour of those two Divine Imperial Regalia.

From the Divine Age, besides those religious personages, certain hereditary corporations claimed the exclusive privilege of charge of the State Shintō rites: They are the Nakatomi, the Imbe, and the Sarume families, and later on the Urabe family was added to these. So the customs and manners of religious communities of ancient Japan remind us more or less of those of Samoa, where "the father of the family carries on the ancestor cult. With regard to the gods of villages, it is said that 'the priests in some cases were the chiefs of the place ; but in general some one in a particular family claimed the privilege, and proposed to declare the will of the god. His office was hereditary'" (W. J. Perry, *Children of the Sun*, p. 191).

V PHYSICAL AND MORAL PURITY, AND
THE IDEA OF SIN

In ancient Shintō documents, such as the *Kojiki*, the *Nihongi*, the *Norito*, and the *Kogoshūi*, the idea of sin is still of a nature more physical than moral. The Heavenly and Earthly Offences enumerated in the olden *Norito* or *Shintō Rituals* in the *Engishiki* are mostly physical in nature. The Heavenly Offences are those of breaking down the divisions of the rice fields, filling up the irrigating channels, opening the flood gate of the sluices, sowing seed over again, erecting rods in the rice fields, flaying animals alive or backwards, spreading excrement over the doors. The Earthly Offences are wound-defilement, corpse-defilement, albinos (lepers), excrescences (warts or corns or bunions), incest, bestiality, calamity through crawling worms or grubs, calamity sent by the Thunder-God on high, calamity through birds in the air, destruction of other people's domestic animals, and magical incantations (*Vide* K. A. Florenz, the English translation of the *Ōharai-no-Norito. T. A. S. J.*, Vol. XXVII).

In examining the nature of the offences mentioned above, the reader will readily see that, excepting incest, they are all physical and yet not moral.

Likewise, the idea of purity and impurity is merely physical. In ancient Shintō documents purity meant ritual purity; and impurity, uncleanness or pollution, is, as a rule, of a physical nature. Therefore corpses are impure; blood is unclean. If a person has, even by chance, touched them his body must be purified with due ceremony.

For instance, when Izanagi returned from his visit to the land of Death, he did not lose any time before purifying himself with water of lustration by plunging into the stream of a small river (*E. T. K.*, p. 39). As death is a pollution, Ajisuki-Takahikone-no-Kami was offended at being mistaken for a dead friend, Amewakahiko (*E. T. N.*, Vol. I, p. 67). The God Izanagi of the Island of Awaji sent a curse upon the Emperor Richū on account of blood defilement which displeased the God (*E. T. N.*, Vol. I, p. 307). Yamatotakeru princeps imperatorius, ab orientali sua expeditione domum rediens, Atsutae, in oppido Owari quae appellatur provinciae, versabatur cum coniuge Miyasuhime, cuius fascia menstruationis sanguine erat inquinata ita, ut ipse quoque inquinaretur. Therefore, it seems to me that he, when he went up Mt. Ibuki to crush the evil mountain deity there, could not take the Divine Kusanagi Sword with him for fear of its being defiled, and left it behind with Miyasuhime [1] (*E. T. K.*, p. 215), and the result was his destruction by the mountain demon, since he was bereft of the supernatural protection of the Divine Sword.

Sickness, particularly pestilence, to the simple-minded people of ancient Japan, was a calamity inflicted upon them through evil influences of unseen powers. It was imagined as being sent by the Evil Deity, Ōmagatsumi, the Japanese Ahriman. People must be careful of being cleared of it. Thus they had in consequence the great purification ceremony. They must ward off the evil deities of sickness, so they had the

---

[1] Cf. *Owari-no-Kuni-Atsuta-Daijingū-Engi* or *Kambyō-Engi*. *Vide* G.R.k., Vol. I, p. 856.

Michiaematsuri or Festival of the Road Deities, already mentioned. These Road Deities really, however, are nothing but the evil deities of pestilence, whom people wish to prevent from entering the capital. Such bad influences from the evil deities must be got rid of, so it has become customary that small dolls in paper or in metal are made, and, carrying people's sins committed daily, they are thrown adrift into a river or sea. These dolls are called an agamono or ransom, —an inanimate scapegoat, we might say. In 706 (the 3rd year of Keiun), for instance, an epidemic disease raged, from which deaths were countless, so a great ceremony of exorcism was held for the first time at the capital of Kyōto (*Shoku-Nihongi*, Vol. III. *K. T.*, Vol. II, p. 43; *Fusōryakki*, Vol. V. *K. T.*, Vol. VI, p. 538). On such an occasion the effigy of an ox, in clay, is the medium or ransom object, carrying away people's misfortunes.

Thus different sorts of incantation, witchcraft, spell, magic, curse, divination, are abundantly mentioned in old Shintō documents.

As we have seen above, ancient Shintō has no morality to speak of; even the idea of purity is mostly ritualistic and physical. And yet the germ of ethical religion is not quite lacking in ancient Shintō. Besides its prohibition of incest and bestiality, it has two kinds of ordeal which, with an entire absence of the idea or at least without a presentiment of moral order in the world, could not have arisen. The two kinds of ordeal are by boiling liquid and by fire. It is recorded that the first case of ordeal took place in the reign of the Emperor Ingyō, when His Majesty ordered the rectification of falsities or corruptions of heraldry in family traditions by having the person concerned plunge his hand into a caldron of boiling water placed on the Amakashi Hill, and then call on his deities to witness (*E. T. N.*, Vol. I, p. 316. *Cf. Shinsen-Shōjiroku, Preface*).

The ordeal by boiling water is called "Kugadachi"[1] or "Putting one's hand in boiling water," and it cannot exist without an idea of moral law or order governing the world—a presentiment of the agreement of the moral order and the physical order of the world.

Next let us pass to ordeal by fire, and examine how it came to be in ancient Shintō.

According to the *Nihongi* tradition, Konohana-no-Sakuyahime suffered this fire ordeal in order to prove her chastity, when the Heavenly Grandson Ninigi-no-

---

1 Besides the two kinds of ordeal alluded to above, the *Nihongi* mentions two other kinds of ordeal. One is an ordeal by boiling mud and the other an ordeal by an axe heated red-hot (*Vide E. T. N.*, Vol. I, p. 317). According to some Japanese philologists the word *Kugadachi* is derived from the Korean words *kuk* and *chat* (Ueda and Kanazawa, *Nihon-Gairaigo-Jiten*).

Mikoto, her husband, suspected her of being unfaithful to him, as the Indian Rāma did to his innocent wife Sītā, because Konohana-no-Sakuyahime told him that she became pregnant through lying with him for a single night (*E. T. N.*, Vol. I, p. 88).[1] In this case the underlying moral principle is the same with that of the boiling water ordeal in the reign of the Emperor Ingyō.

The religious custom of calling one's deities to witness is referred to in other records. Examples are frequent not only in the *Nihongi* but also in several other books of later times, *e. g.*, the *Heike-Monogatari*, the *Taiheiki*, the *Azumakagami*, etc. It is the origin of the kishōmon or written oath by the deities, very common among the samurai or warriors of the Middle Ages of Japan. So, in the *Nihongi* we read in the reign of the Empress Saimyō (*d.* 661) that an Ainu, Onka by name, made oath by the Deities of the Bay of Aita[2] that the Ainu there would serve the Imperial Government with pure heart (*E. T. N.*, Vol. II, p. 252). A similar incident took place among the Ainu in the reign of the Emperor Bitatsu (537–585). In this case the Ainu made a pledge by calling to witness the God of Mt. Mimoro, *i. e.*, Ōnamuchi-no-Kami (*E. T. N.*, Vol. II, p.

1 *Cf.* The *Zappōzōkyō* or *Samyuktaratnapiṭaka-Sūtra* (Nanjiō's *Catalogue*, No. 1329).

2 The present Akita.

97). A similar case of Aïnu oath is found in the *Shōtoku-Taishi-Denryaku* or *Biography of the Crown Prince Shōtoku.*

When the Emperor Tenchi (614–671) was about to die, the Government officials pledged allegiance to the Crown Prince Ōtomo by invoking different deities, both national and foreign, Shintoistic or Buddhistic (Brahmanistic), to witness. The form of the oath runs thus :—

"If any of us should disregard them (the Emperor Tenchi's commands), let the Four Heavenly Kings smite him, and let the Gods of Heaven and Earth moreover punish his offence. Let the thirty-three Devas bear witness to this" (*E. T. N.*, vol. II, p. 298).

W. G. Aston comments in his foot-note of the *Nihongi* :—

"There is here a curious mixture of Brahmanism, Buddhism, and Chinese religion. Curiously no reference is made to the Shintō God" (*ibid.*).

In my opinion, however, the expression, "Gods of Heaven and Earth," in the oath, includes, beyond question, Shintō deities.

In the reign of the Emperor Bitatsu, the Ainu made oath, as mentioned above, saying :—

"If we break this oath, may all the Gods of Heaven and Earth, and also the Spirits of the Emperors, destroy our race."

Here it may be with good reason asserted that by the Gods of Heaven and Earth Shintō deities are not excepted (*E. T. N.*, Vol. II, p. 97). The Gods of Heaven and Earth invoked in the oath of the Ainu are not very different from those of Shintō.

The following words of the Imperial Prince Yamashiro-ōe, son of the Prince Regent Shōtoku (574–622), also referred to the Gods of Heaven and Earth. Invoking them to witness, he said :—

"I am simply declaring what I have heard, and I call to witness to its truth the Gods both of Heaven and Earth" (*E. T. N.*, Vol. II, p. 161).

This half religious and half social custom of making pledges by deities became more and more in vogue among the warriors from the 12th century (in the Gempei Era) onward, and actual examples are too many to quote here. The expression kishōmon or a note of pledge is very familiar to us in the literature of that period and afterwards.

PART II SHINTŌ IN THE STAGE OF ETHICO-INTELLECTUALISTIC RELIGION

CHAPTER XI

DAWN OF INTELLECTUAL AWAKENING

The most primitive peoples are not conscious of the Laws of Nature or Cosmic Order, *i.e.*, they are not aware of the fact that Nature is not a chaos but a Cosmos. Consequently they believe that daily occurrences are due to the caprice of deities. The Bechuanas of South Africa, for instance, cannot recognize Cosmic Order and do not believe that the sun sets, but that he dies every day. Certain tribes of Australia believe that the sun kills the moon every month. The Basutos believe that the moon is clever enough to escape the sun's chase when she is reduced to a mere thread and gradually recovers her former shape (*Vide* D'Alviella, *Hibbert Lectures on the Origin and Growth of the Conception of God,* p. 166).

According to Dr. W. J. Perry, Maori ancestors believed that the moon dies and returns again to this world (W. J. Perry, *Children of the Sun,* p. 210).

The ancient Egyptians believed that Osiris, the

sun, is killed by the demon of darkness in the evening every day, and as the new sun, Horus, he is reborn and rises the next morning.

In the consciousness of these primitive peoples everything in Nature is governed by divine caprice, and not by regular recurrence; *ipso facto* that there is no order in Nature, or no inviolable laws of Nature; no causality, either physical or moral. In the long course of development of human culture, however, men by degrees became conscious of the existence of something which science calls Cosmic Order or Natural Law, something unchangeable in things changeable, something immutable and inviolable in things mutable and violable by the will on the part of men. The seer of the *Rg Veda* was conscious of this truth and sang of the God Indra thus :—

"The sun and the moon move in regular succession in order that we may believe, O Indra!" (I, 102, 2)

The Greek poet Pindar also says :—

Νόμος ὁ πάντων βασιλεὺς θνατῶν τε καὶ ἀθανάτων

(Platon, *Gorgias*, § 87).

Thus the rta of Vedic India, the Persian Asha, the Egyptian Maat, and the Greek Moira came into existence.

In Japanese mythology, when Konohana-no-Sakuya-hime, the consort of the Heavenly Grandson Ninigi-no-Mikoto, became pregnant in a night in nuptial relations with her husband, the Prince exclaimed :—

"How is it possible for me, Heavenly God though I am, in the space of one night to cause anyone to become pregnant ? " (*E. T. N.*, Vol. I, p. 88)

This amounts to saying that such a thing as abrupt pregnancy is beyond man's power, it is quite super-human or supernatural ; nay, it belongs to the category of miracles, *i. e.*, against Natural Law. So, in my opinion, here we cannot fail to discern in Japanese mythology a dim beginning of the consciousness of Natural Law which ancient Japanese had found for themselves by the time of the formation of the myths mentioned in the *Kojiki* and the *Nihongi*.

In the Emperor Yūryaku's Edict at his demise, we find that he considered death as the inevitable "common lot of all humanity" (*E. T. N.*, Vol. I, p. 370), whereas in the Divine Age there is the case of the dead Amewakahiko, whom his wife, children, and relatives seem to have tried to recall to life by means of crying and singing songs.[1] Therefore it is quite natural that there was a magical Jewel, " Makarukaeshi-no-Tama," mentioned in the ancient document *Kujiki*, by means of which the dead are believed to be restored to life. The Emperor Yūryaku's Edict cited above, at once

---

[1] *N. B.* It is a well-known fact that with some Australian aborigines there is no belief in natural death. They suppose a man dies because an evil agent kills him. *Vide* Gilbert Murray, *Five Stages of Greek Religion*, 2nd edition, p. 38. Also Lévy-Bruhl, *Primitive Mentality*, pp. 38, 41, 63.

reminds us of the Greek idea of Fate, whose decree, even Zeus, the divine father of Sarpedon, could not violate. So we read in Homer :—

"Woe, woe ! that Fate decrees my best-belov'd,
Sarpedon, by Patroclos' hand to fall"

(*Iliad*, XVI, 501, 502).

"Yet not the Gods themselves can save from death
All-levelling, the man whom most they love,
When Fate ordains him once to his last sleep"

(*Odyssey*, III, 305–306).

Simonides of Ceos also says :—

'Ανάγκη οὐδὲ θεοὶ μάχονται.

The *Heike-Monogatari* breathes the same spirit of the necessity of causal nexus :—

"The sound of the bell of Gionshōja echoes the impermanence of all things. The hue of the flowers of the teak tree declares that they who flourish must be brought low. Yea, the proud ones are but for a moment, like an evening dream in spring time. The mighty are destroyed at the last, they are but as the dust before the wind" (A. L. Sadler's English translation of the *Heike-Monogatari*. *T. A. S. J.*, Vol. XLVI, Part II, p. 1).

It goes without saying that here the Buddhistic idea of Karma, the necessary law of causality or retribution, is predominant both in the physical and the moral world.

Greatly influenced by this Buddhistic idea of Karma, the Emperor Gomizunō (1596–1680) writes :—

" And if even the Buddha of the three worlds cannot escape the Law of the Impermanence of all things, how can mere man hope to do so ? "[1] (*Kochō*,[2] A. L. Sadler's English translation, p. 7).

So, the Emperor Hanazono (1297–1348) in his autographical diary remarks :—

" Life or death, the Fate alone ordains. Even Deities cannot interfere "[3] (*II Shinkishū*, p. 315. *Vide Ressei-Zenshū*).

In this stage of development of religious culture men came to classify deities by the category of true and false. Thus in the *Nihongi* we read that a certain intelligent Koromonoko, refusing to be sacrificed to a river-god, plunged two calabashes into the stream, and said :—

" O thou River-God,.... If thou dost persist in thy desire to have me, sink these calabashes and let them not rise to the surface, then shall I know that

---

1 *Cf.* The *Daihatsu-Nehangyō* (Skt. *Mahāparinirvāṇa-Sūtra*) :—

" All the Tathāgatas, though their bodies, like a diamond, are indestructible, are subject to the law of impermanence, myself of course not being an exception. This is the true law of the universe applicable to all the Buddhas. Such being the case, never break out into tears of sorrow and lamentation, though death may at once separate me from you " (Nanjiō's *Catalogue*, No. 118).

2 Published by the Meiji Japan Society in Tōkyō in 1922.

3 A well-known Greek proverb says :—

" What the Fate has written on her tablet, no axe can cleave."

thou art a *true God*, and will enter the water of my own accord. But if thou canst not sink the calabashes, I shall, of course, know that thou art a *false God*, for whom, why should I spend my life in vain ?" (*E. T. N.*, Vol. I, p. 281)

Yamaga-Sokō, the founder of Bushidō and a great scholar of Chinese classics in the Tokugawa Regime, severely criticised the immoral act of sacrificing human beings to the River-God in the reign of the Emperor Nintoku from the standpoint of Chinese philosophy and ethics and said :—

" In my humble opinion, offering a human sacrifice to a demon is a custom of the barbarians. It cannot please a true deity, because he refuses to be worshipped with such a false offering. The Emperor Nintoku did wrong in offering a human sacrifice to the River-God, although it was required in the Emperor's dream. In this respect, wise ruler as he was, he was by far inferior to the sagacious Koromonoko, who could tell a true deity from a false " (*Chūchō-Jijitsu*, Vol. II, *Seisei*).

According to a certain legend, the Māra or Buddhist Satan, fearing that Buddhism might become the most influential religion of Japan, asked Amaterasu-Ōmikami of the Ise Shrine, the Greatest Deity of the national religion of Japan, that she would obstruct the propaganda of Buddhism in this country, and then he would, in return, protect her Imperial descendants. The compact thereupon entered into between Amaterasu-Ōmikami and the Buddhist Satan seems to have been faithfully observed by the Goddess, although she was not altogether averse to the Buddhist faith. The Buddhist priest Shiren, a famous biographer of Japanese Buddhist priests, in the 14th century, criticised the above legend, saying :—

"If the Great Goddess of the Ise Shrine took the side of the Buddhist Satan against the true religion of Gautama Buddha, she might be called a false (evil) deity and not a true (right or good) deity" (*Genkōshakusho*, Vol. XVIII. *K. T.*, Vol. XIV, p. 945).

Here again we see that the Deity is placed in the logical or ethical category of true (good) or false (evil).

Fujiwara-no-Tsuneaki of the 14th century put the same ethico-religious truth as follows :—

"The God of Mount Kasuga's Shrine doth teach
The Way of Truth Sincere, to all and each,
As Heaven's first law; which, cherished in my heart,
Shall hold me faithful till with breath I part"

(*Shinshūi-Wakashū*, Vol. XVI).

CHAPTER XII

DETHRONEMENT OF MINOR DEITIES AND AMALGAMATION OR UNIFICATION OF DIFFERENT DEITIES

As we have seen above, nearly all natural objects were deities to the ancient Japanese. So, the tree was a deity, the serpent was a deity, even a small insect was a deity. But there appeared a new tendency in which such deities of nature religion gradually lost their divine dignity or prerogative and at last were degraded or dethroned.

In the reign of the Empress Suiko, we are met with an instance. Under an Imperial order to build ships, Kawabe-no-Omi, disregarding admonishings by the people, felled trees on mountains sacred to the Thunder-Deity. Then it thundered very violently, but the Thunder-Deity—a deity in nature religion—could do no harm to Kawabe-no-Omi, because he did what he ought to do as a loyal subject under the command of the Empress, who was a Deity by far superior to the divine Thunderer, a deity in the natural stage of the Shintō religion (*Vide. E. T. N.*, Vol. II, p. 147).

In the reign of the Emperor Nintoku, legend says, there was a water-snake in a river in Kibi Province, which was feared as the divine owner of that river, and was a great and dangerous nuisance to persons travelling in the locality, because it belched forth poison and injured the passers-by. Hereupon Agatamori entered the river with upraised sword and killed the monster snake, to the great benefit of the people. And thus an evil deity succumbed to the sword of righteous indignation in the interest of the general public (*E. T. N.*, Vol. I, p. 298).

The case is the same with Hata-no-Kawakatsu, who dethroned the Silkworm, reverentially styled, by witches and wizards, the Tokoyo-no-Kami or Eternal Deity, and worshipped by credulous people in the 7th century (the reign of the Empress Kōkyoku). Hata-no-Kawakatsu indignantly killed one of the witches and wizards, and made the others cease from persuading the people to this superstitious worship (*Cf. E. T. N.*, Vol. II, p. 189).

According to one traditional legend, Hitokotonushi, Deity of Mt. Katsuragi, on offending the Emperor Yūryaku, was banished by His Majesty to Tosa Province (*Shaku-Nihongi*, Vol. XII. *K. T.*, Vol. VII, p. 672) and, according to another legend, En-no-Shōkaku, a Buddhist (or Brahmanical) priest and medicine man, inflicted a supernatural punishment upon Hitokotonushi, for belittling him and disobeying his priestly commands, which were intended for the promotion of the weal of the general public (*Genkōshakusho*, Vol. XV. *K. T.*, Vol. XIV, p. 884).

And again, local tradition says that there was a mountain fiend in a secluded part of the country—Itō in Izu Province—who from time to time violently attacked travellers over the Hiekawa Mountain Pass, seizing them and hurling them to their death in the bottomless ravine. In the middle of the 17th century, however, Nichian, the Buddhist Saint of the Butsugenji in Itō, was asked to ward off the demon by means of reciting Buddhist liturgies. In the fulness of time, the virtuous Nichian's ardent prayer of exorcism made the demon desert the place, leaving a message of repentance for his past misdeeds. Unfortunately the message, being written in the superhuman language of demons, is indecipherable. The legend clearly supplies the suggestion that a deity in a lower religion cannot survive the struggle for existence in a higher stage of culture even in circles of superhuman beings and through natural selection is by degrees replaced by a deity of a religion of a higher order in religious development (*Itōshi*).

Therefore Shirai-Sōin gave his critical view on the legend of Hitokotonushi and En-no-Gyōja (or Shōkaku) as follows :—

" I hardly believe the legend, which tells us that Hitokotonushi was conquered by human power, even though he, as a God, ranked aloof from man, because it contradicts the conception of a God, who is and must be higher than man. We are told in one legend that the deities served Shōkaku as a servant serves his master, and, according to another legend, that Shōkaku was banished to a distant land. Thus Shōkaku seems to have been superior to the deities and, at the same time, inferior to man—stories mutually contradictory. It is regrettable that Shintoists should amuse themselves thus in concocting incredible tales both strange and irrational, lacking in discrimination " (*Jinja-Keimō*,[1] Vol. VI).

Now let us proceed to examine how the divine amalgamation or unification in Shintō has taken place.

In the *Shimmyōchō* or *Catalogue of the Names of Shintō Shrines* in the *Engishiki*, we find numerous Ōkuninushi-no-Kami (or Ōkunitama) or Great Divine Lords or Spirits of the Localities,—*numen loci*—for example, the Ōkuninushi-no-Kami (Ōkunitama) of Izumo, the Insular Ōkunitama in Tsushima, the Ōkunitama of Iki, Mutsu, Owari, Ise, and Izumi (*K. T.*, Vol. XIII). It can be easily seen that each of these is in origin a local guardian spirit—though some of them might have been historical personages—attached each to its own place, just as the Ōkuninushi-no-Kami of Izumo is, in that locality, a divine spirit with some historical back-

1 Published in 1667 (the 7th year of Kambun).

ground. But later on the people came to believe that they were all one and the same Ōkuninushi or Ōkunitama or Great Divine Lord or Spirit of Izumo. This is a concrete example of the amalgamation or unification of Shintō deities.

The Deities of Mt. Tsukuba were at first merely a God and a Goddess of that mountain,—simply a deification of the mountain, as a male and a female, in a certain stage of nature religion—but by and by those two mountain deities—probably a product in a comparatively early stage of nature religion—became identified with Izanagi and Izanami, the Divine Couple, well known in Japanese mythology.

The peerless Mt. Fuji, whose name, in its origin, is an Ainu word, meaning " fire " or " Goddess of Fire," was worshipped because the volcano itself was looked up to as an awe-inspiring Deity, but afterwards the Mountain-Deity was identified with Konohana-no-Sakuyahime, the divine consort of the Heavenly Grandson Ninigi-no-Mikoto and a daughter of the God Ōyamatsumi or Great Mountain Spirit in Japanese mythology.

According to the *Shintō-Gobusho* or *Shintō Pentateuch*, Ame-no-Minakanushi-no-Kami or the Divine Lord of the Very Centre of Heaven, Kuni-Tokotachi-no-Mikoto or the Earthly Eternal Divine Being, and Toyouke-Daijin or Miketsu-Kami, *i. e.*, the Food-Goddess and

Divine Waitress to the Ancestral Sun-Goddess Ama-terasu-Ōmikami are amalgamated and otherwise called Daigenshin or the Great Original Divinity (*K.T.*, Vol. VII, p. 431). And, according to the same book, the Great Original Divinity is further identified with Ama-terasu-Ōmikami or the Great Ancestral Sun-Goddess and sometimes called Kokūshin or the Divinity of the Great Void (*ibid.*, p. 477).

In the *Kujiki*, the Sun-Goddess, the Moon-God, Ame-no-Sagiri-no-Kami or the God of Heavenly Mist, Kuni-no-Sagiri-no-Kami or the God of Earthly Mist— these four deities are artificially amalgamated as one Deity, Ame-Yuzuru-Hi-Ame-no-Sagiri-Kuni-Yuzuru-Tsuki-Kuni-no-Sagiri-no-Mikoto (*Kujiki.* Vol, I. *K. T.*, Vol. VII, p. 173), just as Zervanem Akaranem—the personi-fication of "limitless time," the unifying principle of Ahura Mazda and Ahriman in Persian religion—became the Supreme Unity under the Sassanides, though the germ of this conception was already found in the *Avesta* (Count D'Alviella, *Hibbert Lectures on the Origin and Growth of the Conception of God*, p. 226).

A similar process of unification of deities took place in the field of Greek religion likewise. The Orphic verse says :—

"Zeus, Hades, Helios, and Dionysos are one"
(George Moore, *History of Religions*, p. 591).
And, Julianus also says :—

" Zeus, Hades, Dionysos are one and are Serapis "

(*ibid.*).

In Vedic India the rsi or poet sings :—

" Oh, Agni, thou art born Varuna, thou becomest Mitra when kindled ; all the gods are in thee " (v, 3, 1).

" Indra, Mitra, Varuna, Agni, for the poets give many names to the one " (i, 164, 46).

Thus, in a certain stage of its development, the unification process takes place in all religions.

In mediæval Japan as the local governor newly appointed could not make a round of pilgrimage to each and every shrine in the locality under his governance, he adopted a new plan of establishing a shrine called " Sōsha," meaning a shrine dedicated to the whole of the deities in his district, and for convenience' sake [1] worshipped here, at one time, all the local deities ; just as at Agora in Greece one altar was dedicated to many deities all together, and one particular altar was erected in honour of the 12 Olympic deities by the family of Pisistratos of Athens (Chantepie de la Saussaye, *Lehrbuch der Religionsgeschichte*, 3. Aufl. Bd. II, S. 314).

So in a Japanese poem composed by Tatchimon-in we read :—

[1] Ban-Nobutomo, *Jinja-Shikō*, Vol. I (*Collected Works*, Vol. II, pp. 53, 54).
Hirata-Atsutane, *Tamadasuki*, Vol. V (*Collected Works*, Vol. IV, p. 213')

" Though each Divinity its shrine doth claim,
And rev'rent worshippers their off'rings make;
Still, guided by the undivided twain,
The world its single way doth safely take "
(*Shin-Zoku-Kokin-Wakashū*).

As Shintō more and more responded to Buddhist influences, the Sun-Goddess Amaterasu-Ōmikami became identified with one of the great Buddhist Divinities, Mahāvairocana,[1] the Dainichi or Great Sun; and Ōnamuchi (*i.e.*, Ōkuninushi-no-Kami) and Sukuna-hikona-no-Kami were identified with the Buddhist Deity Yakushi (Skt. Bhaiṣajya-guru-vaiḍūrya-prabhāsa) in the Shintō of the Ōarai-Isosaki Shrine in Hitachi Province (*Shimmyōchō* in the *Engishiki. K. T.*, vol. XIII, p. 336).

Similarly, the statue of the War-God Hachiman of the Tōdaiji at Nara made by Kaikei (or Kaikyō) in the year 1201 (the first year of Kennin) is nothing but a Buddhist priest in shape. According to Nissen, the Buddhist priest of the Nichiren Sect, the statue of the Deity of Kasuga represents the complete unification of Shintō, Confucianism, and Buddhism, because the statue is in Buddhist apparel, holds a jewel[2] in its hand and

1 This beginning of amalgamation is already discernible in the *Diary* by a certain Nobuhira, a Shintō priest of the Ise Shrine, a contemporary of the famous Buddhist priest Kōbō in the 9th century (*Vide Tōdaiji-Yōroku. Z. Z. G. R. K.*, Vol. XI, p. 7).

2 The reader may well remember that in ancient Shintō the jewel was a talisman or fetish.

wears a cap of Chinese style (*Banshin-Engiron*, Vol. II, p. 50).

Shintō and Buddhism, first conflicting, by degrees came into friendly contact, and at length into complete union, and the result has been the syncretism of Shintō and Buddhism. Here arose the Ryōbu (Dual) Shintō or Amalgamated Doctrine of Shintō and Buddhism, the Sannō-Ichijitsu Shintō (the One True Shintō of Mt. Hiei), the Ise Shintō (the Shintō of the Ise Shintō priests), the Yui-ichi Shintō or Unamalgamated Genuine Shintō, etc. The fundamental principle of the Ryōbu Shintō is the idea of the relation of the Original (or Noumenal) and its Appearance—the Honji-Suijaku.[1]

As early as the reign of the Emperor Seiwa (850–880), the Buddhist priest Eryō proclaims :—

"The Kingly Buddha educates men, revealing the Truth, sometimes in a part, sometimes as a whole. The Great Bodhisattva incarnates himself in a Deity or a Sovereign" (*Nihon-Sandai-Jitsuroku*, Vol. III. *K. T.*, Vol. IV, p. 42).

Buddhas are the originals or prototypes in Heaven whereas Shintō Deities are their earthly counterparts or manifestations on earth. They are one and the same in origin, the only difference being in their appearances.

1 We cannot fail to see the same amalgamation or unification process in the Nō Literature. *Vide* W. Gundert, *Schintoismus im Japanischen Nō-Drama* (*Mitteilungen der Deutschen Gesellschaft für Natur-und Völkerkunde Ostasiens*), Bd. XIX, S. 196, 198.

Therefore, Minamoto-no-Yoshiyasu of the Tokugawa Regime says :—

"All the Heavenly and Earthly Deities, the Ancestral Deities, Mountain-Deities, and Sea-Deities are nothing else but different manifestations of the Fundamentally True One. Therefore they are all manifestations of Mida (Skt. Amitāyus and Amitābha) or Dainichi (Skt. Mahāvairocana). For this reason, and others, in the doctrine of both Tendai and Shingon Sects, we are met with the True Original One from which spring all the different Shintō Kami manifestations" (*Ryōbu-Shintō-Kuketsnshō,* vol. v, p. 13).

In the same spirit Fujiwara-no-Saneyasu (1270–1327) says :

"With Gratitude and Hope we recognize
That all the Sacred Shintō Shrines we prize
Are but reflections of Celestial Light
Bestowed on humble earth by Heavenly Skies"

(*Gyokuyōshū*).

Minamoto-no-Michichika (1149–1202) also sings :—

"Unnumbered Deities, with Heavenly Love,
Their unseen help have promised from above;
Assuring Buddhas' grace in lifetimes three—
The Past, the Present, and the Yet to be!"

(*Sengohyakuban-no-Uta-Awase*)

Thus far we have seen the doctrine that the Buddha is the original or the true, while the Kami or Shintō Deity is nothing but its temporary manifestation. The

Japanese religious mind could not stop here; on the contrary, it tried to proceed in a reverse direction and asserted that the Kami or Shintō Deity is the original and the true, and Buddhas are but its derived manifestations in disguise.

Urabe-no-Kanetomo (*d.* 1511) was the chief champion who advocated this doctrine thus :—

" Exoterically speaking, the Buddhas are the original and the true, the Shintō Deities are the humble earthly manifestations of the celestial Buddha. Esoterically considered, however, the Shintō Deities are the original and the true, the Buddhas are only disguised manifestations on earth " (*Yui-ichi-Shintō-Myōhō-Yōshū*.[1] *Z. G. R. k.,* Vol. III, p. 650).

The Buddhist priest Sōji represents the same school of Shintō religious thought, saying :—

" Since the Kami or Shintō Deities are the original and the true, and the Buddhas are only their manifestations, the secular law of the State is the law divine, *i. e.,* the Way of the Deities, there being no difference at all between the State law and the religion of the Buddha ; Shintō and Buddhism are one and the same, the spiritual and the temporal are by no means different, and thus both being united in one, they join in the service of the nation with harmony and unanimity " (*Saiten-Kaifushō*).

[1] This book is ascribed to Urabe-no-Kanenobu, but most native scholars are of the opinion that the real author is Urabe-no-Kanetomo.

CHAPTER XIII

FROM POLYTHEISM TO PANTHEISM WITH SOME PHASES OF HENOTHEISM AND MONOTHEISM

Shintō is in its origin polydemonistic and then polytheistic, and its crude philosophy, as we have seen, is animism. The next stage in the line of its development shows an aspect of naturalistic pantheism, greatly influenced, particularly later on, by Mahāyana Buddhism. We can discern the germ of naturalistic pantheism in Shintō even in its oldest documents. As, for instance, some trees are produced from Susano-o's divine body, in other words, those natural objects are after all portions of one and the same divine body of the God Susano-o. In the *Nihongi* we read :—

"So Susano-o-no-Mikoto plucked out his beard and scattered it [about]. Thereupon Cryptomerias were produced. Moreover, he plucked out the hairs of his breast, which became Thuyas. The hairs of his buttocks became Podocarpi. The hairs of his eye-brows became Camphor-trees" (*E. T. N.*, Vol. I, p. 58).

In a similar way, the *Nihongi* records, animals and plants sprang from the corpse of the Food-Goddess Ukemochi.

"On the crown of her head there had been pro-

duced the ox and the horse; on the top of her fore-
head there had been produced millet; over her eye-
brows there had been produced the silkworm; within
her eyes there had been produced panic; in her belly
there had been produced rice; in her genitals there
had been produced wheat, large beans and small beans"
(*E. T. N.*, Vol. I, p. 33).

Again the *Nihongi* mentions that Susano-o the
Storm-God, Amaterasu-Ōmikami the Sun-Goddess, and
Tsukuyomi-no-Mikoto the Moon-God sprang, respect-
ively, from the nose and the left and right eyes of
Izanagi. In this case, also, natural objects, such as the
sun, the moon, and the rainstorm, are nothing but
divine offspring of one and the same God Izanagi
(*E. T. N.*, Vol. I, pp. 27, 28).

The Chinese legend of Pan-Ku[1] shows some faint
trace of naturalistic pantheism, which has a resemblance,
though in a crude form, to the myths of the birth of
the so-called "Three Noble Children"[2] of Izanagi.

[1] In the Japanese reproductions the legend of Pan-Ku runs as
follows :—

"In a certain foreign country, was a giant called Pan-Ku. When he
stretched out his arms to their full length, the sky came into existence;
when lying down, the earth. His eyes, when open, became day-light;
when shut, the darkness of night prevailed. He was 80,000 years of age.
When he died, his two eyes became the sun and the moon; his bones
became rocks and minerals, his blood made the rivers, and his hairs trees
and herbs" (*Shaku-Nihongi*. Vol. V. *K. T.*, Vol. VII, p. 583). *Cf. E. T.
Kg.*, pp. 91, 92.

[2] *I. e.*, the Sun-Goddess, the Moon-God and the Storm-God.

This at once reminds us of the crude pantheistic philosophy of the *Gedō-Shōjō-Nehanron* in describing the God Mahesvara. It runs as follows :—

" The God Mahesvara—the ethereal heaven is his head, the earth is his body, the water is his urine, the mountains are his excrement, all the living beings are worms in his belly, the wind is his vital breath, the air his bodily heat, both good and evil are the Karma or constituents of his character " [1] (Nanjiō's *Catalogue*, NO. 1260).

Thus, in ancient Shintō, as we have seen above, animism made its appearance first, followed by a stage of the naturalistic pantheism of Shintō. This is clearly seen in the book entitled the *Nijū-Issha-no-Ki* or *Notes on the Twenty-One Shrines*, whose alleged author is Kitabatake-Chikafusa, the noted statesman and great scholar in the 14th century :—

" Our country is begotten of the Divine Couple, the Divine Male and the Divine Female. Therefore the mountains, the rivers, the trees, and the herbs have their own divine names. So the Mountain-Deity is called Ōyamatsumi, the Water-Deity Mizuha-no-Me, the Sea-Deity Watatsumi-no-Mikoto, the Deity of Streams

---

[1] Also notice the same strain in the *Mundaka Upanisad* (II, 1, 4) :—
" Fire is His Head, His eyes sun and moon,
His ears the regions of the sky,
The revealed Veda is His voice,
The wind His breath,
The Universe His heart, from His feet is the earth.... "

Haya-Akitsuhi-no-Mikoto, the Deity of Mud Haniyasu, the Deity of Fire Kagutsuchi, the Deity of the Wind Shinatobe-no-Mikoto (or Shinatsuhiko), and thus in every cloud of dust or in each little particle of the natural elements there is a deity inherent. In what the eye can reach, in what the ear can hear, in what the hands and feet can feel, we are everywhere, in amazement, met with Divinity. The Sun-Goddess in the sky shines by day while the Moon-God sheds light upon us by night. The former is no other than the Ancestral Goddess Ōhirumemuchi-no-Mikoto[1] while the latter is called Tsukuyomi-no-Kami. As Shinatobe is the Wind-Deity, it is the air, the breath of the universe, and at the same time the breath of each person, which is to say that a man living in this world is inhaling and exhaling the divine air or holy spirit, therefore he should be reverentially careful even of his respiratory functions."

Thus we see that this author's elucidation of Shintō theology none the less reveals an aspect of naturalistic pantheism—a transition from animistic polytheism to naturalistic pantheism. So Urabe-no-Kanekuni says :—

> " E'en in the single leaf of a tree,
> Or a tender blade of grass,
> The awe-inspiring Deity
> Manifests Itself "

[1] *I.e.*, Amaterasu-Ōmikami.

(*Kanekuni-Shintō-Hyakushu-Kashō.*

Z. G. R. k., Vol. III, p. 699).

The oracular utterance ascribed to the Awaka-Daimyōjin breathes the same spirit :—

" Béhold the azure sky,
  The mighty vault o'er all ;
  While here the softly blowing breeze
  Swaying the myriad pine-wood leaves
  Plays Nature's own sweet air,
  In Nature, God's glory shines.''

The Buddhist priest Tada-Kōsen of the 19th century says of the pantheistic aspect of Amaterasu-Ōmikami :—

" Spring flowers and autumn leaves !
  Emanations all are they
  Of that bright light divine,
  By Heaven's radiant Goddess shed
  Upon this Earth to shine ! ''

In the poem of the Emperor Kōkaku (1771–1840) we read :—

" The vital food of which we daily eat,
  No less the raiment that we don, so fine,
  And e'en the smallest motes our eyes that meet—
  All own the governance of Law Divine ! ''

The Shintō theologian Tachibana-no-Sanki of the Tokugawa Regime also says :—

" In each of the three wondrous worlds of life—
The past, the present, and that yet to come—
The first before our birth, the second now,
The next to open when we breathe our last—
Through all are we maintained by Grace Divine ! "

The theme of the last quoted stanza at once reminds us of the striking expression of St. Paul, " We
live, and move, and have our being in Him " (*Acts*,
XVII, 28), in which we can see a germ of pantheism
in the Pauline Christianity. And thus, in the course
of its development, the polytheistic phase of Shintō
gradually passes into a pantheism.

As we have just seen, although the animistic
polytheism of original Shintō evolves into naturalistic
pantheism, Shintō, in its progress, is by no means
lacking in an aspect of henotheism or monotheism.
Hence, Imbe-no-Hironari, the author of the *Kogoshūi*,
found a henotheistic aspect of Shintō apparent in
Amaterasu-Ōmikami or the Ancestral Sun-Goddess,
regarding whom he said :—

" Now since Amaterasu-Ōmikami is the greatest
Ancestral Goddess, no other Shintō Deities can claim
equality, just as a son is ever inferior to his father,
or a vassal to his lord " (*E. T. Kg.*, p. 46).

The author of the *Heike-Monogatari* also says :—

" This was the Shrine of the Sun-Goddess who
descended in ancient times from the Plain of High

Heaven....incomparable and pre-eminent among the deities of the 3,780 greater and lesser shrines of the 60 provinces of Nippon " (*Heike-Monogatari. Vide T. A. S. J.*, Vol. XLIX, Part I, p. 38).

Izawa-Nagahide went a step further and propounded the monotheistic doctrine of Shintō as follows :—

" The God Kuni-Tokotachi[1] is one and at the same time the 800 myriads of deities. It is the One Great Common Root of Heaven and Earth ; all things in the universe are in this One God ; from the beginning of the universe to its very end, the God Kuni-Tokotachi exists everlastingly " (*Shintō-Ame-no-Nuboko-no-Ki. S. T.*, p. 239).

This rendering by Izawa-Nagahide recalls Cleanthes' hymn to Zeus :—

"Most glorious of immortals, many named,
　　　　　　　　　　　　powerful over all,
　　Zeus, thou author of all nature, guiding
　　　　　　　　　　　　all with law,
　　Hail to thee " (Clifford Moore, *Religious Thought of the Greeks*, p. 193).

In the *Reikiki* falsely ascribed to Kōbō, we read:—

" The Deities at both Shrines of Ise have neither beginning nor end, the Great Original Divinity, incomprehensible, transcending our thought " (*Z.G.R.k.*, Vol. III, p. 132).

---

[1] The Earthly Eternal Divine Being.

The author of the *Miryū-Shintō-Kuketsu*, strongly influenced by Buddhist philosophy, says of Amaterasu-Ōmikami, the original Sun-Goddess :—

" Amaterasu-Ōmikami is the True Body of the Primordial Buddha, all-pervading, ever-present, having neither beginning nor end " (*Miryū-Shintō-Kuketsu*, Vol. II).

In the *Shintō-Gobusho*[1] or *Shintō Pentateuch* we also read :—

" It is the Void, that is the Spiritual Existence, the Incorporeal Unity, revealing Itself in thousands of forms.... We call it Ōhirumemuchi or Amaterasu-Ōmikami. This is the Noumenal Essence of all kinds of things in the phenomenal world " (*Gochinza-Hongi. K. T.*, Vol. VII, p. 460).

---

[1] As the book consists of five parts it may, not inaptly, be termed the " Shintō Pentateuch ". From evidence furnished by the text it seems probable that compilation was made in the thirteenth century by some Shintō priests attached to the Outer Shrine of Ise.

CHAPTER XIV

ANCIENT MYTHS AND THE THREE DIVINE IMPERIAL REGALIA: AN ATTEMPT AT RATIONAL INTERPRETATION

As the Japanese mind became intellectually self-awakened, it ceased to satisfy itself with the ancient myths as they were handed down; it became self-conscious that they contradicted themselves and could no longer be believed as before.

Tanikawa-Kotosuga, a very critical-minded scholar, in the Tokugawa Regime, felt keenly the need of giving a new interpretation to the ancient myths, and advanced a hypothesis that they bear two significations, one literal (*sensu proprio*) and the other symbolical (*sensu allegorico*), in support of which he instanced, from the *Nihongi* myths, the pass called "Yomotsu-Hirasaka" or the "Even Pass of Hades" between this world and another, which the God Izanagi and the Goddess Izanami traversed in their descent to the Underworld or Hades.

Sensu proprio, we must admit that according to some tradition there was, in the province of Izumo, such a pass—"Yuyasaka" by name. This is on one hand what is called by Tanikawa-Kotosuga the "literal meaning " of the ancient myth, but on the other hand we must bear in mind that " Yuyasaka " has a figurative or symbolical meaning, according to which it implies a man's breathing his last (*Nihonshoki-Tsūshō*, Vol. I, *Preface*).

In the same manner, Kawamura-Hidene tried to explain away all the difficulties, illogical and irrational, in the myths, and to give a figurative interpretation to them. One of the *Nihongi* tales is that, when about to be delivered of a child, Toyotamahime transformed herself into a crocodile or dragon ; but, according to Kawamura-Hidene, this fable must be taken only in a figurative manner, the true sense being nothing more than allegorical expression of Toyotamahime's labour pains in childbirth (*Shoki-Shūge*, Vol. II, p. 35).

Kamo-Norikiyo (*d.* 1861), of the Tokugawa Regime, is one of the champions who made the best use of such allegorical interpretation, and attempted to derive from the myths moral teaching that might satisfy the advanced ethical consciousness of a religious teacher of that period. He interpreted figuratively the passage of the *Nihongi* according to which the Emperor Jimmu met with almost unsurmountable difficulties in leading his troops on his expedition to the eastern district, because his enemy were numerous and obstinate in the way. Kamo-Norikiyo says that the enemy were not ordinary visible flesh-and-blood foes standing up against us ; they were, rather, all within ourselves—invisible, impalpable, inward foes, very hard to overcome. When the Emperor Jimmu was to cross the rugged mountain pass of self-hood in mental darkness, Kamo-Norikiyo's Ancestor Kamotaketsunumi-no-Mikoto, by command of Amaterasu-Ōmikami, appeared to him in the bodily form of a large crow and served as his mental guide (*Shintō-Uden-Futsujoshō*, Vol. I).

The case is the same with Imbe-no-Masamichi, when we have his famous view of myths as follows :—

" Our ancient tradition is a great teaching full of truth : it expounds the phenomenal by the noumenal or the noumenal by the phenomenal. The mind yet in crude infancy seeking after the true and the divine expresses itself only in its own simple and plain words " (*Shindai-Kuketsu, Preface*).

To put this in Schopenhauer's terminology, the ancient Japanese myths may not be true in *sensu proprio*, but in *sensu allegorico* they contain the nucleus of eternal truth.

From the same standpoint Empedokles interpreted Zeus in the ancient myths of Greece as another name of fire; Hera, the divine wife of Zeus, wind ; Hades, earth ; Nellis, water.

Theagenes also says that Athene is wisdom, Ares recklessness, Aphrodite passion.

Some Japanese interpreters of the ancient myths

did not stop here, but went on to discredit the myths as merely " olden time jokes for the children's amusement,"[1] with no real meaning, just as Platon called the Greek myths " noble lies," Euripides scornfully termed them "the minstrels' sorry tales," and Herakleitos attributed them to a " sacred disease," or as did one of the greatest modern scholars of mythology and religion, Max Müller, a production of the " disease of language."

The Divine Mirror, Sword, and Jewels are the Three Divine Imperial Regalia and they were regarded by the ancient Japanese as a kind of talisman or charm, or something like fetishes. But as men's minds intellectually and morally awoke the Three Divine Imperial Regalia took an ethical significance, imbued with symbolical meaning. So Kitabatake-Chikafusa, who wrote a Japanese history, entitled *Jinnō-Shōtōki*, said :—

" The Mirror reflects from its bright surface every object as it really is, irrespective of goodness or badness, beauty or the reverse. This is the very nature of the Mirror, which faithfully symbolizes truthfulness, one of

---

1 Tachibana-no-Moribe, *Izu-no-Chiwaki. Collected Works*, Vol. I, p. 86.

Cf. When the Emperor Chūal met a certain Itote in Tsukushi, Itote presented the Emperor with the mirror, sword, and jewels saying :—

" As to these things which thy servant dares to offer, mayst thou govern the universe with subtlety tortuous as the curvings of the Yasaka Jewels ; may thy glance survey mountain, stream and sea-plain bright as the Mirror of white copper ; mayst thou, wielding this ten-span Sword, maintain peace in the Empire " (*E. T. N.*, Vol. I, p. 221).

the cardinal virtues. The Jewel signifies soft-hearted-
ness and obedience, so that it becomes a symbol of benevolence. The Sword represents the virtue of strong
decision, *i.e.,* wisdom. Without the combined strength
of these three fundamental virtues peace in the realm
cannot be expected " (*Jinnō-Shōtōki,* Vol. I, p. 20).

The Buddhist priest Nikkō published a book on
Shintō, written from the standpoint of the Nichiren
Sect, entitled *Shintō-Dōitsu-Gemmishō,* and said of the
Three Divine Imperial Regalia :—

" These three symbols—Confucianism calls them
Wisdom, Benevolence and Courage[1]: the Mirror sym-
bolizes Wisdom, the Jewel Benevolence, the Sword
Courage. In Buddhism, they are styled the Three
Categories of truth—the Category of the Void represented
by the Sword, that of the Transient or Phenomenal by
the Mirror, the Category of the Moderate by the Jewel.
We must remember that the Perfect Way, *i.e.,* the
Middle Path, is the " Wondrous Law " or the True
Religion of the Buddha."

Ichijō-Kaneyoshi (or -Kanera) followed Kitabatake-
Chikafusa in giving a new signification to the Three
Divine Imperial Regalia. Thus philosophized he :—

" The Three Divine Imperial Regalia are the

[1] In Dr. Baty's symbolical language these three are Stainlessness,
Sweetness and Valiance respectively (Thomas Baty, *Shintō* in the *Hibbert
Journal,* Vol. XIX, No. 3, p. 421).

essence of Shintō tenets and the fundamental principle of the Imperial rule ; the final fusion with Confucianism and Buddhism, thus interpreted, is not entirely alien to the Japanese mind. The essential element of Confucianism, Buddhism and Shintō has its existence in our mind: there is no Truth apart from our mind ; we cannot find Truth outside our mind. The mind is Divinity, Truth is the Way. The three teachings are after all one and the same thing. The selfsame One is manifested in a threefold way. Thus considered, the Three Divine Imperial Regalia symbolize one and the same Mind " (*Nihonshoki-Sanso*, Vol. II, p. 42).

The Buddhist priest Shiren in the 14th century attributed a grand symbolical meaning to the Three Divine Imperial Regalia, when he said :—

" Of things, natural or artificial, one is to be preferred to the other, all the world over. Historically considered, our country has arisen of itself naturally— it was not established artificially or by a human device ; wherein lies, of itself, the uniqueness of Japan, quite differing from any foreign country—China, for instance. The Mirror, the Sword, and the Jewel, the Three Divine Imperial Regalia, are quite natural, with nothing of an artificial character.... And thus, symbolized by the Divine Insignia, has ensued our Imperial lineage unbroken and coeternal with Heaven and Earth " (*Genkōshakusho*, Vol. XVII. *K. T.*, Vol. XIV, pp. 922–925).

CHAPTER XV

GERMS OF MORAL IDEAS IN SHINTŌ AND APPEARANCE OF A CHANGE IN THE IDEA OF SACRIFICE

In my opinion Aston may be right in saying that ancient Shintō has no moral teachings to speak of. The germs of morality, nevertheless, can be found in some of the traditions of the *Kojiki* and the *Nihongi*. For instance, when the God Susano-o was to visit his divine sister Amaterasu-Ōmikami in Heaven, the latter was greatly alarmed and thought that her impetuous brother Susano-o had "no good intent" and it was only that he wished to wrest her land from her (*E. T. K.*, p. 45). When the God Susano-o protested, Amaterasu-Ōmikami demanded of him to prove the "sincerity of his intention" (*E. T. K.*, p. 47). Here we have the expressions "good intent" and "sincerity" of heart. This implies no other than the germs of moral ideas in ancient Shintō.

In the *Ōharai-no-Norito* or *Ritual of the Great Purification* incest[1] together with bestiality was explicitly prohibited.

---

[1] *Vide* K. A. Florenz, *Ancient Japanese Rituals*, *T. A. S. J.*, Vol. XXVII, Part I, p. 61.

The ancient Japanese were already conscious that it is a virtue to keep one's word. So the breaking by Izanagi[1] of the promise made to his divine wife Izanami caused him to be deprived of his consort, never to be restored, just as the renowned mythical Greek poet Orpheus forever lost his beloved wife Eurydike through breaking his oath sworn before the infernal King Pluto.

The existence of germs of morality may easily be proved, as I have mentioned above, by the fact that some kinds of ordeal were already familiar among the ancient Japanese.

Now let us see how this seed of morality grew into the great tree of the Shintō ethical system, under which birds of the air may find rest for themselves.

As already shown, there is evidence that some forms of human sacrifice existed in ancient Japan. As is the case everywhere else, a process of attenuation in human sacrifice took place at a certain stage of civilization. Arai-Hakuseki, a noted scholar and statesman in the Tokugawa Regime, mentions in his brief history of the Loochoo Islands that it was quite customary for the people there to worship the Sea Deity, Obotsukakuraku-no-Kimmamon by name, when he got angry, by breaking their arms and pulling out their nails, in order to appease him (*Ryūkyū-Kokujiryaku. Collected Works,*

[1] *E. T. K.,* pp. 35, 36.

Vol. III, p. 662). They did so, because they wished to sacrifice, not the whole human body, but only some portions of it, on the principle of a part instead of the whole.

The annual festival still observed at the Kō-no-Miya Shrine, dedicated to the Owari-Ōkunitama or Local Guardian Spirit of Owari Province, reminds us of a Shintō cult of expiatory human sacrifice of olden times (a piacular rite), and exorcism inseparably connected therewith. In this case nowadays we find a human scapegoat—the φαρμακός of the Japanese Thargelia—carrying all evils of the year with him and being driven out after thrice circumambulating the sacred pavilion temporarily erected and attached to the shrine. In remote antiquity, it is highly probable that the ceremony involved a real human victim.[1]

According to a tradition handed down to and preserved by the Tame family,[2] in ancient times the local governors used to send a certain number of human scapegoats as tribute to the Imperial Court, for use on behalf of the Emperor. It is uncertain whether these scapegoats were actually slain as a means of preserving

1 *Owari-Meisho-Zue.*
Kurokawa-Harumura, *Shimmyōchō-Kōshō-Dodaifukō* (Ban-Nobutomo, *Collected Works*, Vol. I, p. 654).
Shintō-Myōmoku-Ruijushō, Vol. V, p. 9.
Mano-Tokinawa, *Shinka-Jōdan*, Vol. III. *S. T.*, p. 188.
2 Hirata-Atsutane, *Koshiden*, Vol. XXIXa, p. 26. *Collected Works*, Vol. IX.

the life of the Emperor, but it may with some reason be supposed that there was a real human victim, who took the place of the sovereign himself.

A similar case of attenuated human sacrifice is traditionally reported in the *Bōsō-Shiryō* :—

" Anciently human sacrifice was offered to the :ity of Sakato, but in later days the person to be ıcrificed having been chosen by lot, the Shintō priest ,f the Shrine presented the victim to the Deity, on ;he chopping board, alive, as if the person had been actually killed on the spot. Tradition says that the ill-fated one allotted to be sacrificed would assuredly die within three years. This remarkable ceremonial usage, however, is now quite out of practice."

In the *Tosa-Nikki*, a mirror,[1] instead of a human victim, was offered up by the boatmen to appease the Sea-Deity when divine wrath was revealed through a sudden gale of wind which, in the Inland Sea, overtook a vessel having on board Ki-no-Tsurayuki, the famous 10th century provincial governor and poet, and threatened him with shipwreck and drowning.

The Buddhist priest Dōshō (629-700), on his way home from China, was overtaken by a sudden storm at sea, and when it was ascertained by divination that

---

1 In the *Tosa-Nikki* it runs as follows:—"'Let me give to the god my mirror,'....No sooner had I done so than the sea itself became as smooth as a mirror" (Aston, *History of Japanese Literature*, p. 74).

the Sea-Deity, greedily covetous of a saucepan, a religious treasure, which Dōshō was bringing from China, had sent the storm in order to obtain it, the priest was constrained to offer the precious article in appeasement, whereupon the storm ceased and Dōshō reached Japan in safety (*Honchō-Kōsōden*, Vol. I. *B. Z.*, p. 65).

The Buddhist priest Gan-an, while sailing on a certain lake, suddenly encountered a storm so violent that he despaired of escape from it. But he appealed to the Buddhist Goddess Kannon[1] (Skt. Avalokiteśvara) and offered up prayers to her, by virtue of which the wind and waves subsided (*ibid.*, Vol. XLVI. *B. Z.*, p. 642).

Although these last two instances are somewhat of a legendary nature, they show that men's minds in a certain stage of religious development became conscious of the horridness of bloody human sacrifice and tried to abolish it, more or less under the influence of Buddhist and Confucian ethical teachings.

The same idea is dramatically and graphically described by a writer called Jukakusai as follows :—

" In ancient times there dwelt in Lake Asaka a monster serpent to whom human sacrifice was annually offered up. Tradition tells that on a certain occasion a young girl, Sayo by name, was about to be made the victim and preparations for her sacrifice were in hand on the lakeshore. The poor girl, however, though

---

1 In Chinese Kuanyin.

otherwise helpless, was an enthusiastic devotee of Kannon, the Goddess of Mercy, and she proceeded, in earnest and pathetic tones, to recite the Kannon-Sūtra[1] to the Water Demon. The girl's recital was so successful that the monster serpent was appeased and deserted the lake forever. And thus human sacrifice there was permanently done away with " (*Tōgoku-Ryokōdan*, Vol. I).

Not human sacrifice alone but animal sacrifice as well became incompatible with the religious consciousness of the Japanese, enlightened both by Buddhist precepts of universal benevolence and by Confucian ethical teachings.

The Buddhist Saint Ippen (1229–1289) persuaded the Shintō priests attached to the Mishima Shrine dedicated to the Great Mountain-Deity Ōyamatsumi in Iyo Province not to sacrifice fishes and birds as divine offerings, because the undesirableness of such offerings had been revealed to the Saint through a divine oracle (*Ippen-Shōnin-Nempuryaku. Z. G. R. k.*, Vol. IX, p. 218).

According to the *Ruiju-Fusenshō* (Vol. I), similar animal sacrifices had been usual in the Shintō rites of the Munakata Shrine in Kyūshū, erected to the three Goddesses, Ichikishimahime, Tagorihime and Tagitsu-

---

1 *Avalokiteśvara-Bodhisattva-Samantamukha-Parivarta of the Saddharmapundarika* (Nanjiō's *Catalogue*, No. 137).

hime, born at the time of an oath between Amaterasu-Ōmikami and Susano-o-no-Kami. But during the 10th century, under the potent influence of the Buddhist faith consequent upon the amalgamation of Shintō and Buddhism through the Goddesses being indentified with the Bodhisattva, the Government prohibited them, and thereafter the Dharma (Buddhist religion) was brought as a spiritual offering while flowers and incense-burning became the innocent material objects presented to the Goddesses at the Shrine (*K. T.*, Vol. XII, p. 1093).

However striking and powerful the Buddhist influence upon Shintō was, the time-honoured religious customs and usages once solidified in Shintō in its stage of nature religion could not be fully eradicated. Animal sacrifice still survived and was preserved in the Shintō rites, for instance, at the Itsukushima Shrine of Aki Province or the Suwa Shrine of Shinano Province in the 13th century. By way of giving a far-fetched explanation of such bloody offerings from the standpoint of the causal nexus of Buddhist Karma it was declared that animals sacrificed to the Shintō Deities would, instead of being damned in Hell eternally, surely be re-born on earth from time to time, until they were finally saved by virtue of merit acquired through their being sacrificed to Celestial Beings—so did the Buddhist monk Mujū-Hosshi of the Kamakura Period solve the paradoxical religious riddle.[1]

---

[1] Mujū-Hosshi (-Hōshi), *Shasekishū*, Vol. I, p. 19. Sakauchi-Naoyori, *Honchō-Shosha-Ichiran*, Vol. VIII (*Z. Z. G. R. K.*, Vol. I, p. 380).

This somewhat sophisticated argument on animal sacrifice to the Shintō deities by the Buddhist monk reminds us of a parallelism, though different in language, in Sallustius' defence of the same sacrificial practice in the old Greek religion (*Vide* G. Murray, *Five Stages of Greek Religion*, pp. 227, 261, 262).

CHAPTER XVI

INNER PURITY EMPHASIZED, AND SINCERITY OR UPRIGHTNESS AS THE FUNDAMENTAL ETHICAL PRINCIPLE BECOMES PRE-EMINENT IN SHINTŌ

In the course of development Shintō Deities by degrees came to prefer spiritual offerings to material—just the idea of the offering of the Buddhist Dharma, because Heavenly and Earthly Deities subsist on the *Hokkekyō* or *Saddharmapuṇḍarīka-Sūtra* and find the source of spiritual strength in uprightness, as proclaimed Nichiren, the founder of the Buddhist Nichiren Sect (*Nichiren's Epistle to Hōjō-Tokimune. Ibun* or *Posthumous Works*, p. 608).

So, in the second year of the Kemmu Restoration (1335), when the loyal Kusunoki-Masashige believed that unseen aid from the Shintō Deity had enabled him to destory the entire hostile Hōjō army, he presented to the Shintō Deity of a certain shrine, as a spiritual offering, an autograph copy of the *Hokkekyō*.

The *Miryū-Shintō-Shodaiji-Bushū*, a book on the Dual Buddhistic Shintō, giving instruction to pilgrims to the Ise Shrine, embodies a stanza which is reproduced in the following translation :—

" Blessed are they that, 'gainst the hour of need,
Take refuge in the Goddess, and their meed
Of off'rings pure her shrine do place before;
For she, in her good grace, rewards will pour."

The anonymous writers of the *Shintō-Gobusho* say:—
" What pleases the Deity is virtue and sincerity, and not any number of material offerings " (*K. T.,* Vol. VII, p. 457).

This beautiful teaching of Shintō vividly recalls the prophetic voice of Euripides as well as the well-known protest of Hosea against animal sacrifice then in vogue in Israel.

Euripides exclaims :—

Εὐ ἴσθ' ὅταν τις εὐσεβῶν θύῃ θεοῖς κἂν μικρὰ θύῃ τυγχάνει σωτηρίας.

The Hebrew prophet Hosea says :—
" I desire mercy and not sacrifice " (*Hosea,* VI, 6).

We are also familiar with the same protest against offerings material instead of spiritual, by the Stoic philosopher Seneca who, like Hosea, says :—
" The divine nature is not worshipped with the fat bodies of slain bulls, or with gold or silver votive offerings, or with money collected for the sacred treasury, but with a pious and upright will " (Clifford Moore, *Religious Thought of the Greeks,* p. 200).

The ethical teaching of Shintō mentioned above

is very close to that of the writer of the Book of Proverbs :—

" To do justice and judgment is more acceptable to the Lord than sacrifice " (XXI, 3).

Inoue-Masakane (1790–1849), the founder of the Shintō Misogi Sect and afterwards a poor forlorn exile in Miyake Island in the Pacific off the coast of the province of Izu, says :—

" Have steadfast faith in the Deity, and ye attain the spiritual felicity by him afforded. The worldly-minded erroneously value gold and silver and other earthly goods—fiefs—as precious treasures, only to find, with regret, that they are transient and soon gone. Assuredly they cannot bring true spiritual consolation to the soul ; they cannot afford to a family or to a country any happiness or comfort worthy of the name ; they never supply mental satisfaction " (*Yuiichi-Mondō-no-Sho-Kakitsugi*).

This exhortation of the exiled Shintō prophet, as he may well be styled, recalls a celebrated passage in the *Epistle of St. Paul to the Romans* :—

" The Kingdom of God is not meat and drink ; but righteousness, peace, and joy in the Holy Ghost " (*Rom.*, XIV, 17).

And it also reminds us of the Beatitude :—

" Blessed are the poor in spirit : for theirs is the Kingdom of Heaven " (*Mat.*, V, 3).

The Imperial Prince Kane-akira (914–987) writes in the same sense :—

" Gods or Spirits are impartial and just in mind, pleased only with a man's religious piety. Approach and pray to them with a sincere heart, and be sure that you will thus gain their favour ! " (*Honchō-Monzui*, Vol. XIII, p. 1).

Yamaga-Sokō, the well-known founder of Bushidō or the Japanese " Warrior's Way," says in his *Chūchō-Jijitsu* :—

" The surest passport for entrance into communion with the Divine is Sincerity. If you pray to the Deity with Sincerity, you will assuredly realize the divine presence."

Sincerity thus, once for all, emphasized as an ethical principle in Shintō, there appeared a change in the conception of " Purity " and " Impurity," one of the fundamental ideas of Shintō. The *Shintō-Gobusho* explains the meaning of " Purity " and " Impurity " from the ethical point of view, as follows :—

" To do good is to be pure ; to commit evil is to be impure. The deities dislike evil deeds, because they are impure " (*K. T.*, Vol. VII, p. 478).

The Emperor Meiji (1852–1912), whose religious sentiment oftentimes found expression in a national poem composed by His Majesty himself, wrote as follows[1] :—

---

[1] I have taken the liberty of reproducing Prof. F. A. Lombard's English translation of the original poem from his book *Imperial Japanese Poems of the Meiji Era*.

" With the unseen God,
    Who seeth all secret things,
        In the silence—
    Communes from the earth below,
    The heart of the man sincere."

An old song to accompany a divine pantomimic dance runs thus :—

" By what gay art shall we essay
    The Goddess of the Sun to please,
    That she may still vouchsafe her ray,
    Nor leave us, in dark gloom to grieve ? "

In explaining the meaning of what is here rendered as " gay art " Tachibana-no-Moribe (1781–1849) understands simply the pantomimic dance by Ame-no-Uzume-no-Mikoto in front of the Heavenly Rock-Cave, when the Sun-Goddess concealed herself therein—a theatrical performance of no very decent kind in the naturalistic stage of Shintō (*Kagurauta-Iriaya*, Vol. III. *Collected Works*, Vol. VII, p. 86).

Tachibana-no-Sanki went a step further and commented on the same song, attaching an ethical significance to it, when he says :—

" Man's good heart reflects the Divine Will of the Sun-Goddess. By ' gay art ' is meant the ethical supreme good, just the golden mean between two extremities, conformable to reason. This is also the

Divine Good " (*Shintō-Shihon-Engi.   S. T.*, pp. 156, 157).

Ichijō-Kaneyoshi (1402–1481) emphasizes the inner significance of purity and says :—

" There are two significations of purity in Shintō : one is outer purity (bodily purity) and the other inner purity (purity of heart).   If a man is truly sincere in mind he will be sure to succeed in realizing a communion with the Divine.   This is no other than inner purity or Sincerity, which means purity of heart or uprightness of heart " (*Nihonshoki-Sanso*, Vol. II, p. 112).

Tomobe-no-Yasutaka, of the Tokugawa Regime, often known as Yaegakiō, also says :—

" What is ablution ?   It is not merely the cleansing of one's body solely with lustral water, it means one's following the Right and Moral Way.   Pollution means moral evil or vice.   Though a man wash off his bodily filth, he will yet fail to please the Deity if he restrain not his evil desires " (*Shintō-Shoden-Kuju. S. T.*, p. 324).

This argument reminds us of the Oracle of Apollon at Delphi :—

" To the pure precincts of Apollo's portal,
    Come, pure in heart, and touch the lustral wave ;
    One drop sufficeth for the sinless mortal ;
    All else, e'en Ocean's billows, cannot lave."

And Epicharmos preaches the same truth, thus :—

" If thou art pure in mind, thou art pure in thy whole body."

Inner purity or purity of heart in worshipping the Sun-Goddess at the Ise Shrine is exceedingly emphasized by Saka-Shibutsu in the diary of his pilgrimage to that shrine in the year 1342. He says :—

" It is quite customary for us neither to bring any offering to the Goddess nor to carry rosaries about us like Buddhists. In short, we have nothing special wherewith to recommend ourselves in petitioning her Divinity. This is the true signification of inner purity. Washing oneself in the sea-water, and being cleansed of the bodily filth—this is outer purity. Being pure in mind and body, our soul is at one with the Divine, and, divinity in humanity thus realized, there remains no desire unsatisfied—there is no occasion for further petition or prayer to the Goddess. This is the true esoteric meaning of worshipping the Sun-Goddess at the Ise Shrine. Being thus enlightened by the Shintō priest of the shrine, I was overwhelmed with a sense of pious joy, and burst into tears of gratitude" (*Daijingū-. Sankeiki. G. R. k.*, Vol. I, p. 982).

Similarly, in one of the Triple Oracles from the Three Shrines,[1] as they are called, the Sun-Goddess revealed herself :—

[1] The Three Shrines are sacred to the Sun-Goddess, the God Hachiman, and the Deity of Kasuga, respectively.

" Although, at first sight, honesty may seem to be unprofitable to man, yet remember that in the end it brings him Sun and Moon's reward." [1]

The *Yamatohime-no-Mikoto-Seiki* in the *Shintō-Gobusho*, probably compiled in the 13th century, says :—

" Prayer is of the foremost importance in appealing for the Divine Grace ; and uprightness is a fundamental quality in one who would obtain the unseen protection. Although the Sun and Moon continually circle round the four quarters, and illuminate every corner of the globe, yet do they unfailingly shine upon the heads of the upright " (*K. T.*, Vol. VII, p. 496).

The Buddhist priest Shiban (1626–1710) emphasizes sincerity and justice or righteousness as the moral principles of Shintō :—

" All the Deities are noble, just and upright, thoroughly impartial in mind ; so they will heed the prayers only of those who also are just and sincere of heart " (*Honchō-Kōsōden*, Vol. LI. *B. Z.*, p. 704).

Kamo-Norikiyo (*d.* 1861), the founder, in the Tokugawa Regime, of the Uden Shintō, afterwards exiled as a heretic to Hachijō Island, proclaims :—

" Prayers to the Deity accompanied by monetary gifts secured by injustice are sure not to be granted. Pray in all righteousness and the Deity will be pleased

[1] The original author of these Triple Oracles was probably Urabe-no-Kanetomo. They first appeared in the *Umpo-Irohashū* in 1548.

to listen to your supplication. Foolish is he who, in impatient eagerness and without following the path of righteousness, hopes to obtain divine protection" (*Shintō-Uden-Futsujoshō*).

This beautiful religious idea of the Shintō priest of the Kamo Shrine at once reminds us of St. Paul's ethico-religious phrase : "the unleavened bread of sincerity and truth" (*I Cor.*, v, 8).

Thus we see that Sincerity or Uprightness, like the principle of Universal Love in Christianity or that of Unconditional Benevolence in Buddhism, became a fundamental tenet of the Shintō religion in the ethico-intellectualistic stage of its development. In an oracle of the God Hachiman we read :—

"I am none but Benevolence Itself. Sincerity is my own divine body" (*Jingishōjū*).

The Oracle of the Deity of Sumiyoshi (or Suminoe) also says :—

"I have no corporeal existence, but Universal Benevolence is my divine body. I have no physical power, but Uprightness is my strength. I have no religious clairvoyance beyond what is bestowed by Wisdom, I have no power of miracle other than the attainment of quiet happiness, I have no tact except the exercise of gentleness" (*Tōshōgū-Goikun*).

A devotee of the same Deity expresses himself thus :—

" Responsive to sincerely offered prayer,
   Full of Sympathy and Pity, will be
   The Deity in Suminoe,
   To one and all, friends or foes,
   Granting heavenly blessings freely "
   (*Jinja-Inshin. Shugendō-Shōso*, Vol. I, p. 346. *N.D.*).

In the same way the Emperor Meiji admonishes
us :—

" Whereas I deem this as an age
   Wherein the world in brotherhood is bound :
   How is it that the fierce winds rage,
   And dash and spread wild waves around ? "

Thus we see a glimpse of religious universalism,
which was introduced into Shintō when the Shintō
Deity was included in the ethical category of Sincerity
or Benevolence ; just as the religious universalism of
the Israelite prophets made its first appearance in the
wake of their religious moralism as soon as the prophets
recognized Yahweh as the hypostatized *Summum Bonum*
of their ethico-religious teachings.

CHAPTER XVII

ETHICAL TRANSFORMATION OF THE NATURALISTIC PHALLIC DEITIES FROM A HIGHER RELIGIOUS POINT OF VIEW AND SOME SHINTŌ RITES OR CEREMONIES MORALIZED

As we have seen above, phallicism was very popular in ancient Japan. Recent finds of relics prove that it existed not only in prehistoric times but in the 8th century as an historical fact, because in 1925 was discovered at Fuchi Village in Hikawa-Gun, Shimane Prefecture, the picture of a phallos drawn on the surface of the walls of a tomb, 1,200 years ago—about two-thirds of a century before the date of the earliest documentary reference in the *Kogoshūi* to the existence of a phallic emblem.

In short, phallic worship was widely known throughout the length and breadth of the Empire from ancient times to modern. But the Japanese minds enlightened by Buddhistic philosophy and Confucian ethics became unable to adhere to the old vulgar beliefs, and then ensued different stories in discredit of abominable forms of nature worship, one of the results being the transformation of phallic deities.

According to the *Gempei-Seisuiki* (Vol. VII, p. 10),

Fujiwara-no-Sanekata, a court noble of the 10th century, on a journey to the eastern district was about to pass on horseback in front of the sacred gate of the Kasa-jima Shrine dedicated to a phallic deity, when he was admonished by the people of the locality to pay respect to the Deity by dismounting at the gate. Being informed that the Deity was a phallic goddess whose parent god in anger banished her from the old capital of Kyōto on account of her having fallen in love with a merchant, the rational-minded court noble refused to dismount as desired and thereby show respect for a shrine in which an indecent figure was preserved. This historical narration shows that some of the well-educated Japanese had already by that time become so rational and advanced in culture that they could no longer believe in such a gross form in nature worship as phallicism.

The *Konjaku-Monogatari* (Vol. XIII) also informs us that a local phallic deity worshipped in Kii Province was converted from its degraded form of divinity by listening to a Buddhist monk, Dōkō by name, who recited the *Hokkekyō*[1] (*K. T.*, Vol. XVI, pp. 731, 732). This story shows that those who embraced a higher religion like Buddhism could no longer find satisfaction in such a crude naturism as phallic worship. This

[1] In Sanskrit, the *Saddharmapundarīka-Sūtra* (Nanjiō's *Catalogue*, No. 134).

being the case, Dōsojin, otherwise named Sae-no-Kami, was easily transformed into the Buddhist Deity Jizō (Skt. Ksitigarbha), as, for example, Koike-Izumo pointed out in his book *Shosaishin-Ryakki*[1] (*J. Z.*, Vol. II, p. 541) in the Tokugawa Regime.

We can, with some degree of reliability, read the past history of phallicism in the stone figures of Dō-rakujizō or the pleasure-seeking Jizō, a divine couple in a posture of coition, in front of the entrance to the Buddhist Temple Tōzen-in in Kanaya-Machi, Tōtōmi Province, and also probably in the Buddhistic Brahmanical divine image of stone in the little Shōden Isle[2] in the pond of Shinobazu near Ueno Park in Tōkyō. In the latter case the stone figure shows no uncommon suspectable aspect when looked at from its front, but the head carefully examined at its back proves to be the *grans penis* of a phallos[3] (*Vide* my Article on the same subject in *T. A. S. J.*, Dec., 1924. *Supplement* to Volume I).

At Mobara-Machi in Chiba Prefecture the older phallic figures were, through the influence of a priest of the Buddhist Nichiren Sect, replaced by a wooden

1 *Cf.* De Visəer, *Acts du IVe Congrès International d'Histoire des Religions*, p. 90.

2 Or, Kangiten (Skt. Gaṇeśa or Vinayaka), a Brahmanical phallic deity.

3 *Cf.* Telesphoros of ancient Greece (Arthur B. Cook, *Zeus, a Study in Ancient Religion*, Vol. II, p. 1090).

image—Mikado-Daimyōjin—in ancient court robe and wearing a ceremonial cap, interpreting the protective phallic deity of marriage between man and woman to be only a humble earthly manifestation of the Celestial Being of Buddhistic metaphysics or the Absolute (*Vide ibid.*).

Almost in a similar way, Yamazaki-Ansai (1618–1682), the founder of the Suika Shintō, promoted Sarutahiko, another phallic deity of ancient Japan, to the rank of a moral teacher who, the learned scholar of Chinese classics believed, preaches the ethical principle promulgated by Amaterasu-Ōmikami, originally the Ancestral Sun-Goddess. The controversy which Hirata-Atsutane raised against Yamazaki-Ansai, accusing him of being guilty of deviating from our time-honoured tradition, very well shows how the moralization of a phallic deity took place in the course of the development of the nature religion of Shintō.[1]

Let us here in passing refer to the " Seven Gods of Luck " in later Shintō, and hear each of them speak on a moral precept :—

(1) The God Daikoku, a dual god of the Indian Mahā-kāla and the Japanese Ōkuninushi-no-Kami (other-wise also pronounced Daikoku) of Izumo Province, says :—

---

[1] Hirata-Atsutane, *Zoku-Shintō-Taii*, Vol. IV. *Collected Works*, Vol. I, p. 101.

  (a) " The man that Perseverance strong,
       Doth ever bear with him along ;
       And who, of his true loyal heart,
       Doth love for parents yield a part ;
       To that man I will freely give
       Of Luck, the best, while he doth live."

  (b) " To shatter rocks in quest of gold
       Is not why I a Mallet[1] hold.
       'Tis meant to rouse by tap upon his head
       The laggard who doth seem his work to dread."

(2) The Deity Ebisu, whose identity has not yet been precisely determined, says :—

    " For generations without end,
      My luck I will bestow—
      On such as sin-ward do not tend,
      But in the Straight Course go."

(3) Fukurokuju, the Taoistic Deity of Happiness, Wealth, and Longevity, says :—

" Who to his inmost heart the Shintō faith doth take,
And Buddha and Confucius his holy guides doth
                        make—
Him will I bless with health, and of world's
                     wealth full store,
And with happy length of life will crown him
                     o'er and o'er."

[1] As regards the Mallet of Daikoku as a charm or talisman, *vide* Aston, *History of Japanese Literature* (p. 213).

(4) The Chinese Buddhist Saint Hotei says :—

"In my protection will I keep,
  The man of peaceful mind ;
Who angry quarrel doth not seek,
  In whose home peace I find."

(5) Benzaiten (Benten) or Sarasvatī, the Goddess of
Streams, Eloquence, and Wealth, says :—

"Take thoughtful heed in all thy daily course,
  To harm no fellow man with angry force ;
Then surely I with wealth will thee reward,
  And o'er thy worldly store keep constant guard."

(6) Another Taoist God Jurōjin, or the Old Man of
Long Life, says :—

"Who to the needy poor, in secret, help doth lend,
And unto those who grieve a pitying eye doth bend—
Him, in the open day, and from age to age his race,
Shall I reward with wealth, and with length of
                                    years, and grace."

(7) Bishamon or Vaiśravaṇa, the Indian God of Wealth
and Treasures, says :—

"Unto the man that useth well the talents Heaven
                                    hath given,
And who far from his honest heart all evil thoughts
                                    hath driven,
My protection I do promise, and on him will bestow
The gifts of health and bounteous wealth in all this
                                    life below."

So much concerning the " Seven Gods of Luck."

Shintō having thus reached the ethico-intellectualistic stage of its development, enlightened believers were no longer able to regard with tolerance ancient fêtes of licentious character such as were held of old in honour of the God and Goddess of Mt. Tsukuba when men and women acted indecently in accordance with their primitive religious customs. The Japanese mind had now awakened to morality of a higher order.

In the Imakami Hot Springs in Shinjō, Dewa Province, a shrine is dedicated to the Deity of Kumano, at which, when cases of fornication or theft occurred near the baths, to the offence of the Deity, the persons implicated, male and female, were strangled, like Laokoon, in the coils of a serpent sent by the Deity to punish them (*Katahisashi-Kōhen. H. Z.*, Vol. Ia, p. 380).

On a festival day each year at the Usaka Shrine, the Shintō priest was wont, in the presence of the Deity, to strike with a stick any woman disloyal to her husband. This was considered as a divine punishment (*Jingishi* in the *Dainihonshi*, the Yoshikawa edition, p. 411. Yoshida-Tōgo, *Dainihon-Chimeijisho*, Vol. II, p. 1964).

In the olden time festival of the Tsukuma Shrine at Sakata-Gun in Ōmi, on the 1st day of the 4th month, every year, a woman to her shame was obliged to put on her head saucepans equal in number to the lovers she had favoured in the course of the preceding year (*Shintō-Myōmoku-Ruijushō*, Vol. V, p. 8). It can be easily seen that the significance of this festival is the prevention of women's unchastity.

So, Government orders, in the 8th century, forbade nocturnal Shintō ceremonies, saying :—

" In the Shintō ceremonies at night men and women get drunk and are licentious with one another, to the injury of public morals. Henceforward Shintō ceremonies should be conducted by day, and not by night " (*Ruiju-Sandai-Kyaku*, Vol. XIX. *K. T.*, Vol. XII, p. 988).

" It is customary that the newly appointed Lord Priests attached to the Izumo Shrine and the Munakata Shrine give orders to the people in their respective parish districts to send to the shrines beautiful maidens of each locality as consecrated waitresses nominally but as concubines in fact. This licentious custom now prevailing under pretext of a Shintō religious rite should be strictly forbidden " (*ibid.*, Vol. I. *K. T.*, Vol. XII, p. 365).

CHAPTER XVIII

WORSHIP OF SHINTŌ DEITIES IN SPIRIT AND IN TRUTH—RESULTING IN ICONOCLASM

As pointed out in the two preceding chapters a great change in Shintō already appeared in the idea of purity and impurity (or filth). Death, in ancient Shintō, is a pollution, blood is a pollution, but in later times they are no longer so considered. Therefore the Buddhist priest Keien (or Kyōen), according to the *Genkō-shakusho,* chancing one day to meet a girl, poor and forlorn, with tears rolling on her cheeks, found on enquiry that, by reason of extreme poverty, she was unable properly to conduct the burial ceremony of her dead mother. Keien out of compassion attended to the matter for the poor girl and the burial rites were duly concluded. Then he repaired to á shrine of the God Hachiman but hesitated to enter, because death being a pollution his intrusion would displease the Shintō Deity. The same evening the God Hachiman appeared to Keien in a dream, commending his observance of the Buddhist ethical principle of Unconditional Benevolence, which induced him to assist the helpless girl to bury the corpse of her dead mother, and told the priest that he might enter the holy precincts without reserve (*K.*

T., Vol. XIV, pp. 839, 840).

A similar incident took place at the Atsuta Shrine in Owari. When the Buddhist priest Shōren whose filial piety induced him to pass by the Atsuta Shrine with the cremated remains of his dead mother in a box on his way to bury them in the sacred Mount Kōya, he refrained from entering the holy place because of the Deity's dislike to the pollution of the ashes. The same night it was revealed in a dream to the Shintō hierophant attending the shrine that a noble guest of honour was about to arrive, whom he must be prepared to welcome. To his surprise he found, in the morning, the Buddhist priest Shōren at the entrance to the Shrine, and him he informed, as directed in the previous night's revelation, that the Deity, being pleased to notice the the filial piety of the priest, was indifferent concerning the death pollution (*K. T.*, Vol. XIV, p. 842).

So the Oracle of the Deity of Kasuga says :—

" If one ceremoniously invited me to his abode by hanging up sacred straw-ropes for thousands of days, yet would I not cross his threshold were he dishonest, harsh or greedy. I am willing to repair to any house, the owner of which has a heart full of compassion and mercy, even though men say he is exceedingly unclean on account of his being in deep mourning for his deceased father or mother ".[1]

[1] There is every reason to believe that this oracle was from the pen

For the same reason blood is not a pollution from the standpoint of higher Shintō, though it displeased the God Izanagi of Awaji Island in primitive Shintō, as is recorded in the *Nihongi* (*E. T. N.*, Vol. I, p. 307).

Izumi-Shikibu, a famous court poetess in the reign of the Emperor Ichijō (985–1011), making a pilgrimage to the Deity of Kumano in Kii Province, while she was unclean (menses), hesitated to approach the precincts of the shrine for fear of defiling the sacredness of the holy place, when an oracular utterance of the Deity gave her permission to enter, saying:—

"Woman, why hesitate,

In lowly sorrow at thy uncleanness,

To come within the gate,

Where dwells unseen the Divine holiness?

Indeed, though spotless, I,

In primal essence of Divinity,

Spurn not in dust to lie,

In fellowship with vile humanity"

(*Fūgashū*).

This divine oracle proves that higher Shintō indisputably transcends the limits of nature religion.

of the Shintō priest Urabe-no-Kanetomo.

Prof. G. Murray speaks of the same trend of religious thought in Greek philosophy after Platen as follows :—

" We find in the religious writings of this period that the real Saviour of men is not he who protects them against earthquake and famine, but he who in some sense saves their souls" (*Five Stages of Greek Religion*, pp. 194, 195).

To the same Deity of Kumano, according to a narration in the *Shasekishū*, once upon a time a lady of great beauty was making pilgrimage when the religious leader of the party became smitten by her charms and made known to her his desire. Greatly perturbed, the lady took counsel of her attendant maid, who loyally determined that in order to protect her lady's honour she would sacrifice her own, and this, under cover of the darkness of night, she actually did. Whereupon the divine anger inflicted immediate death upon the apostate leader as punishment for his thus defiling the sacred neighbourhood of the shrine; whilst, on the other hand, the sin of the maid-servant, having been committed of pure intent and under compulsion, was divinely condoned.

This religious story recalls the Greek legend which tells how, mistaking him for a robber, a man killed his own friend, yet was pronounced by the Delphic Oracle to be innocent—on the ground that the act of homicide was committed through a motive altogether pure and spotless (Fairbanks, *Handbook of Greek Religion*, p. 63).

When Shinra-Myōjin (or Shiragi-Myōjin), the Guardian Deity of the Buddhist Temple Onjōji, was blamed for indifference in having allowed destruction of the temple by fire, the Deity made prompt retort that it was his duty towards true believers of the Buddha's religion to protect them in a spiritual sense, but not to extend protection to material buildings made by mortal hands[1] (*Kojidan,* Vol. V. *K. T.,* Vol. XV, p. 126).

As we have seen above, in the long course of development under the influence of the ethico-intellectualistic religion of Buddhism and of Confucian moral teachings Shintō itself became ethical and spiritualized. So Hayashi-Razan, an eminent scholar of Chinese classics of the 17th century, says:—

"The Deity is the Spirit of Heaven and Earth. The human mind partaking of divinity is a sacred abode of the Deity, which is the Spiritual Essence. There is no Ame-no-Minakanushi-no-Kami (the Divine Lord of the Very Centre of Heaven) apart from the human mind" (*Shintō-Denju. S. T.,* p. 46).

The Buddhist priest Nittatsu (1674–1747) of the Nichiren Sect also says:—

"There is no Deity outside the human mind. Divinity is nothing but spirituality in ourselves....Adore your own divine self by being upright and straightforward, then all the deities will reveal themselves in your mind, and bring happiness and prosperity to you; while a bad man in his disobedience to his own divine self

---

[1] The reader may compare the above with a poem composed by the well-known Kamakura Shōgun Minamoto-no-Sanetomo (*d.* 1219):—

"Not building of great temples, towering up on high,
Nor yet pagodas, graceful, pointing to the sky—
Can Buddha's acceptation earn, even in a little part,
As doth repentance, humble, in the sinner's secret heart"

(*Kinkai-Wakashū. G. R. k.,* Vol. IX, p. 121).

will be damned eternally in the Underworld" (*Shin-Bu-tsu-Myō-ō-ron*, Vol. III, p. 19).

A similar conception of the Deity of a higher order is found in Euripides and the later Pythagoreanism. Euripides says:—

"The mind of each one of us is God".

The later Pythagoreanism also says:—

"God has no fairer temple on earth than the pure soul" (Farnell, *Higher Aspects of Greek Religion*, pp. 144, 147).

Ichijō-Kaneyoshi understands Amaterasu-Ōmikami's worshipping the Heavenly Deities in the Plain of High Heaven, as recorded in the *Kojiki*, to be worshipping her own self-divinity, *i. e.*, the divinity in her mind (*Nihonshoki-Sanso*, Vol. II, p. 158).

The Buddhist priest Jitō of the Tokugawa Regime defines the essence of Divinity as constituted of the attributes qualified as "upright", "pure", "absolute", and "mystico-spiritual" (*Ichijitsu-Shintō-Gen*).

Kaibara-Ekiken (1630–1714), a scholar of Chinese classics, also pointed out the essential attributes of the Deity in terms very similar to those of Jitō, as follows:—

"True, not false, benevolent, upright, all-wise, pure—thus are attributes of the Deity to be reverently thought of. Communion with such a Deity is possible only through the prayer of a man in earnest sincerity, who is himself upright, sincere, and pure in mind"

(*Jingikun. Collected Works*, Vol. III, p. 648).

The alleged author Kitabatake-Chikafusa of the *Nijū-Issha-no-Ki* says of the Japanese Emperor, who was believed to be a Visible Deity in flesh and blood:—

"As a righteous man, pure in mind and just in conduct, is himself a Deity, we understand, in this ethical sense of the words, a Manifest Deity ("Arahitogami" or "Aramikami" or "Akitsukami" or "Akitsumikami")—often mentioned in the Imperial Edicts—in the person of the Emperor" (*Vide S. S.*).

The conception of the Shintō Deity among the enlightened Japanese minds, at a certain stage in the long course of historical development of the religion, was lofty, noble, and spiritual. The consequence is an appearance of iconoclasm in Shintō, because the "Deity is after all incomprehensible, absolute. It transcends the relative principles In (Yin) and Yō (Yang). Therefore we cannot tell what the form of the Deity is." So says the *Zokusajōshō* (*K. T.*, Vol. XII, p. 1406).

In ancient Egypt we find a similar expression of the religious consciousness:—

"He is not graven in marble as an image ...... He is not beheld; .... He is not adored in sanctuaries. .... There is no building that can contain Him......... Vain are all representations" (Renouf, *Religion of Ancient Egypt*, pp. 232, 233).

The Deutero-Isaiah preaches in the same strain:—

"To whom then will ye liken God? Or what likeness will ye compare unto Him?

The workman melteth a graven image, and the goldsmith spreadeth it over with gold, and casteth silver chains" (*Isa.*, XL, 18, 19).

Ise-Teijō (1715–1784), a famous Japanese savant, forbade worship of the Deity by means of statues or images, and said:—

"Never make an image in order to represent the Deity. To worship a deity is directly to establish a felt relation of our heart to the living Divinity through sincerity or truthfulness on our part. If we, however, try to establish a relation between Deity and man indirectly by means of an image, the image will itself stand in the way and prevent us from realizing our religious purpose to accomplish direct communion with the Deity. So an image made by mortal hands is of no use in Shintō worship" (*Gunshin-Mondō. Onchisōsho,* Vol. X).

This passage from Ise-Teijō reminds us of another similar expression of the Deutero-Isaiah:—

"They are all vanity; their works are nothing; their molten images are wind and confusion" (*ibid.,* XLI, 29).

Saitō-Hikomaro (1773–1859) is of the same opinion as Ise-Teijō in regard to the iconoclasm of Shintō (*Katahisashi-Zempen. H. Z.,* Vol. Ia, p. 324).

Shirai-Sōin criticised the two extreme views of the Deity in his book on Shintō, entitled *Jinja-Keimō*, published in 1670, and said :—

"Uneducated people believe to the letter that the Deity dwells in the shrine actually as a man does in his house, whereas men who have the slightest knowledge of philosophy declare that there is in reality no Deity in human form; what faith calls the God Kuni-Tokotachi is, to put it in the terminology of Chinese philosophy, nothing but the Limitless Infinity, and yet the Deity Itself is inherent in the phenomenal, as well. It is I myself that is Divine; besides me there is no Deity at all. We need not adore any anthropomorphic Deity of the Shintō Pantheon. These views mentioned above represent two extremes, whereas the truth always lies in the middle" (*Jinja-Keimō*, Vol. I, *General Introduction*, and p. 4).

"What is the Deity? The Deity is the Absolute. It transcends human words, which are of a relative nature. It is incomprehensible, and yet It permeates all things, It is everywhere. People, as a rule, not knowing this truth, visit a hundred shrines day by day to worship there, and offer a number of valuables month by month, and yet they are not sure to obtain any reward, though they may perchance suffer misfortunes in the world" (*ibid.*, Vol. II, p. 19).

Shima-Shigeoyu, a Shintō priest of the Grand

Shrine of Izumo, in the Tokugawa Regime, therefore says :—

> "Deem not that only in this earthly shrine
>   The Deity doth reign;
>   The earth entire, and all the Heavens Divine,
>   His presence do proclaim!"

Senge-Takazumi (1797-1875), one of the high Shintō priests of the same shrine also sings :—

> "There is no place,
>   On this wide earth—
>   Be it the vast expanse of Ocean's waste,
>   Or peak of wildest mountain, sky-caressed—
>   In which the ever-present power divine
>   In every force of nature's not a shrine."

CHAPTER XIX

SOME DEEPER REFLECTIONS UPON THE DIVINE PROTECTION OF THE NATION—A PROBLEM UNSOLVED FROM THE OLD STANDPOINT OF SHINTŌ, THE NATIONAL RELIGION OF JAPAN

Towards the end of the 11th century and in the course of the 12th a series of civil wars divided the Imperial House into two opposing parties who, with large numbers of samurai warriors on either side, fought several sanguinary battles. Towards the close of the struggle the Heike or Taira clan, guarding the child Emperor Antoku, and bearing, with him, the Three Divine Imperial Regalia[1], retreated from the old capital of Kyōto before the forces of the Genji or Minamoto clan, by whom they were, in 1185, finally annihilated at the naval battle of Dannoura in the Inland Sea, when the infant Emperor was drowned and the replica of the Divine Sword was at the same time lost.

The *Gempei-Seisuiki* tells us of the sad fate of

---

1 Of the Three Divine Imperial Regalia, the Mirror and the Sword were replicas, the true originals being preserved at the Ise and the Atsuta Shrines respectively.

the poor child Emperor Antoku in the following words spoken by his grandmother Niidono:—

"The soldiers are shooting arrows at the august ship, and I have the honour to escort Your Majesty to another one" (*Vide* Aston, *History of Japanese Literature*, p. 143).

In this naval engagement of Dannoura the Heike warriors under the Imperial banner of Antoku-Tennō fought a desperate battle against the fresh strength of the Genji who, in the name of the boy Emperor Goto-ba then crowned at Kyōto under the watchful guidance of the Ex-Emperor Goshirakawa, were ordered to destroy their bitter hereditary foes by the shores of the " Western Sea". Thus, on one side, the Heike family, in support of the infant Emperor Antoku, who was in their charge, were arrayed against their enemies the Genji clan, on the side of the boy Emperor Gotoba.

Immediately after the withdrawal of the Heike army from the capital, Minamoto-no-Yoshinaka[1] came to that city to replace the administration of the Heike by that of his own military forces. The Ex-Emperor Goshirakawa welcomed him and was pleased to furnish him with an imposing guard of honour. But it was not long before quarrels broke out between the capricious Ex-Emperor Goshirakawa and the turbulent warrior Minamoto-no-Yoshinaka—a son of wild nature

1 Otherwise called " Kiso-Yoshinaka ".

brought up in a remote secluded district among the rugged Kiso mountains—the warlike military chief of the "rude barbarians of the distant land", destitute of courtesy and refinement, as they were contemptuously called by the then fashionable and effeminate court nobles of Kyōto. Animosities between the retired Emperor Goshirakawa and Minamoto-no-Yoshinaka reached their climax when the uncultured military leader of the "rude barbarians" recklessly attacked the Imperial Temple Villa Hōjūji, whence the cloistered Emperor Goshirakawa had to flee for his life. The death of Minamoto-no-Yoshinaka, however, which occurred soon afterwards in battle at Awazu in Ōmi, was believed to be a just punishment from Heaven for his disloyalty to the Ex-Emperor.

And, finally, in 1221, when the Imperial party, by order, fought a battle at Uji and Seta with the Eastern forces of the Hōjō, they were utterly defeated, and, in consequence, the Ex-Emperors Gotoba, Tsuchimikado and Juntoku were driven into exile at Oki, at Tosa (afterwards at Awa in Shikoku), and at Sado, respectively, at which places of seclusion they ended their days.

Hereupon, the question naturally arose in the morally awakened minds of the enlightened Japanese of that age:—

"Why was the Imperial army forced to retreat before the 'eastern barbarians', and ultimately destroyed by them?"

To put this in other words, "What caused the sovereign superiors to be beaten by the inferior subjects?"

It is related that before the Dannoura battle, Taira-no-Munemori, of the escort of the child Emperor Antoku, proceeded to Usa, in Kyūshū, and for a whole week prayed the War-God Hachiman, there enshrined, that he would accord victory to the Heike army over the forces of the Genji by whom they were about to be attacked. On the third day of this prolonged appeal, according to the *Heike-Monogatari*[1] record of the incident, the God Hachiman, in an awe-inspiring voice, gave divine oracular utterance thus :—

"No more doth Hachiman at Usa dwell ;
    Nor heeds he now these prayers, belated said;
    Of impious Heike doth sound the knell:
    Reward of arrogance, with justice paid!"
with which ominous oracle, foreboding immediate downfall to the Heike, Taira-no-Munemori and his adherents were greatly dispirited.

Now, what is here set down aroused striking amazement. How should a legitimately reigning Sovereign bearing the Divine Imperial Regalia with him come to sustain so lamentable a fall—unprecedented, certainly, in the annals of the land ? Why should the Heike who,

1   The *Nagato* version of the *Heike-Monogatari* (Vol. XV) published by the *Kokusho-Kankōkai* (p. 511).

throughout, had rendered support to the legitimate Sovereign, suffer destructive defeat; whilst their enemies, in arms against that monarch, though indirectly, gained a victory and with it ascendancy brilliant as the morning sun? Viewed from the old standpoint of the national Shintō religion, in terms of which the Sun-Goddess Amaterasu-Ōmikami and all the other deities had undertaken to defend the legitimate Imperial Sovereign, right or wrong, the circumstances seemed inexplicable.

Among the successive civil wars fought in the 11th and 12th centuries, the disastrous catastrophe of the Shōkyū War mentioned above shook and undermined the ground of the naïve traditional faith in the national Shintō deities, who had vouchsafed to the Japanese nation unconditional divine protection for the people as well as for the Imperial House.

The explanation is very simple. Misfortune fell upon the Emperor—and on his followers as well—because, having become disreputable, from the ethical point of view, they acted against the Divine Will, and the unseen protection of the national deities was in consequence withdrawn from them, with the dire results detailed.

The author of the *Azumakagami*, referring to the unprecedented historical event, the banishment, by their subjects, of the three legitimate Japanese Sovereigns, threw sceptical doubt on the Shintō faith in unconditional protection by the national deities over their Imperial family in particular and the people elect in general of the Divine Kingdom, and said :—

"Amaterasu-Ōmikami, the Ancestral Goddess and Original Ruler of the Land of Effulgent Light or Japan, made a vow everlastingly to protect our august Imperial rulers in their reigns, yet, nevertheless, the Goddess apparently viewed with indifference the unhappy fall of the 85th Emperor and of the two other Imperial rulers who, together with the two Imperial princes, suffered the indignity of being exiled from their beloved capital by the strong-handed measures of the Kamakura Shogunate. This is a matter of great regret as well as utter incomprehensibility!" (*A. K. y.*, Vol. XXIII, p. 176).

The author of the *Masukagami* also admits his inability to solve the enigmatic problem, saying :—

" The fact that the Imperial rulers were overcome in battle by their subjects is unheard of....Despite all expectation that the capital of Kyōto, site of the residences of the reigning Emperor and Ex-Emperors, being divinely defended by Heaven, would be unconquerable, the result proved just the reverse. This is not quite comprehensible without referring to a category not only of the present but of the past merits and demerits of a person, *i. e.*, to the Buddhist doctrine of causal retribution " (*Masukagami. N. B. Z. h.*, Vol. XXIV, pp. 45, 46).

Here we see that the author attempted to solve the enigma confronting Shintō, as the national religion of Japan, by applying the universal doctrine of Buddhistic Karma, which has served very often in the Buddhist religion as a sort of *deus ex machina* in solving questions transcending human ken.

The author of the *Rokudai-Shōjiki,* taking an ethical view, deals with the problem by saying :—

" While disloyalty of subjects means national disgrace, yet the duration and the happiness of an Imperial reign depend upon the Emperor's virtuous government " (*Vide G. R. k.,* Vol. II, p. 416).

Again, from the standpoint both of Confucian ethics and of the Buddhistic doctrine of Karma, Kitabatake-Chikafusa writes to the following purport in his Japanese History *Jinnō-Shōtōki :—*

The defeat of the Imperial Army in the civil war of the Shōkyū (Jōkyū) Era (13th century) may seem an enigmatic riddle —the short-sighted observer will say that there appeared to be no more divine protection over the Imperial family. But, according to the author, the defeat was not owing to discontinuation of the unseen protection from Heaven, it was due solely to lack of moral accomplishment on the part of the Imperial rulers. Minamoto-no-Yoritomo and Hōjō-Yoshitoki had established good government to the satisfaction of the people, whose happiness and comfort they continually endeavoured to promote, and there was no good ground or reason why such benefactors of the country should be destroyed. Since Heaven, as a righteous judge, never helps a man of evil desires and bad conduct, whether he be sovereign or subject, it was natural to expect that the Imperial army should be routed by the forces of the " eastern barbarians ". Although we, Japanese, firmly have devout faith in the national deities and acknowledge the difference *toto cælo* between the rulers and the ruled, likening the one to Heaven and the other to Earth, so that one cannot be replaced by the other, yet neither can with impunity transgress the moral law of good and evil or alter at will the fundamental ethical principle of reward and punishment, *i. e.*, the inviolable law of causal retribution or Buddhist Karma.

The enthusiastic Buddhist monk Nichiren, as a fanatical seer, tried to solve the riddle from the standpoint of his own Buddhistic belief in the *Hokkekyō* or *Saddharmapuṇḍarīka-Sūtra*. He says :—

" The monkish sovereign of Oki Island is a legitimate Imperial Ruler while Gon-no-Tayū[1] is no other than a subject. Why should the Ancestral Sun-Goddess and the God Hachiman permit a son or subject to do harm to his parent or sovereign ? How were the ' eastern barbarians ' enabled to accomplish a feat so extraordi-

---

1   Properly, Sakyō-Gon-no-Tayū, an official title given to Hōjō-Yoshitoki.

nary and incomprehensible as the overthrow of the Imperial Army? The answer is very simple. It was because of the prevalence of the heterodox Buddhist official doctrine of the Shingon Sect" (*Shuju-Onfurumai-Gosho. Posthumous Works*, p. 1407).

Nichiren in his prophetic vision warned the Japanese nation of calamity impending at the hands of the mighty monarch of the Great Mongol Empire, who was about to send an armada[1] against Japan to seal the future destiny of the Divine Kingdom, saying :—

" In the invasion by the Mongols in the 11th year[2] of Bun-ei, not only were a great number of Japanese soldiers killed in battle but the Shrine of Hachiman was destroyed with fire by the enemy. And yet the Mongol Army suffered no divine punishment. Such being the case, it is beyond doubt that the Mongol monarch is greater and mightier than the guardian deities of Japan" (*Kankyō-Hachiman-Shō. Posthumous Works*, p. 2032).

" Owing to the acceptance of the corrupted doctrine of the heterodox Shingon Buddhism, we are about to see a decline of the Imperial rule, leading to the complete destruction of the whole Empire and her subjugation to the yoke of a merciless foreign enemy" (*Honzon-Mondōshō. Posthumous Works*, p. 1803).

" I, Nichiren, was persecuted, wounded with bows

1   This incident took place in 1281.
2   The year 1274.

and arrows and swords, and banished, wherefore the God Hachiman left this sacrilegious land and returned to Heaven, first destroying his abode by fire.... The foreign Power will come and conquer Japan just as a falcon pursues and captures a pheasant, or as a cat kills rats" (*Chimyōbō-Gohenji. Posthumous Works,* p. 2017).

This reminds us of the Israelite prophet Hosea's words, " He shall come as an eagle against the house of the Lord, because they have transgressed my Covenant, and trespassed against my law " (*Hosea,* VIII, 1).
Nichiren continues to speak :—

" Sent by Heaven as a punishment upon the Japanese people, who besottedly adhere to the heterodox Buddhistic Doctrine of the Shingon Sect, warships of the Great Mongol Empire will cross the sea in vast numbers and attack this land " (*Senjishō. Posthumous Works,* pp. 1235, 1240).

This prophetic voice of the Buddhist Saint Nichiren again reminds us of the words of the Hebrew prophets, Isaiah and Jeremiah. Jeremiah, in the name of Yahweh, says :—

" Behold, I will send and take all the families of the North..... Nebuchadnezzar, the King of Babylon, my servant.... will utterly destroy them and make them .... perpetual desolations " (*Jer.,* XXV, 9).

In the same way Isaiah says :—

" O Assyrian, the rod of mine anger, and the staff

in their hand is mine indignation " (*Isa.*, x, 5).

" I will send him against a hypocritical nation, and against the people of my wrath will I give him a charge, ...to tread them down like the mire of the streets " (*ibid.*, x, 6).

The author of the *Hachiman-Gudōkun* admonished the Japanese nation in a strain similar to that of Nichiren :—

" Of old the unseen protection of the Shintō deities and the Buddhas over this land was so effective that invasions of Japan by foreign enemies were at once repulsed. At the present day, alas, owing to evil government, this unseen protection has been withdrawn and the feeble country will now be unable of itself to repel foreign attack " (*G. R. k.*, Vol. I, p. 463).

Notwithstanding all attempts the problem of the divine protection of the realm still remained incompletely solved. Why were the legitimate Japanese Rulers driven to miserable exile in remote regions? What enabled the Kamakura Shogunate to overshadow the hereditary divine right of the Imperial Court of Kyōto? Why did not the tutelary deities of Shintō, the national religion, defend the Imperial family, right or wrong?

Tachibana-Suenari, the author of the *Kokon-Cho-monshū*, aptly applying the doctrine of Buddhist Karma, *i.e.*, the Buddhistic idea of transmigration or rebirth, made an ingenious effort to elucidate the riddle thus :—

" When supplications were presented to the Shrine of the God Hachiman, prayer being offered up throughout the whole night long, a divine oracle gave response in a dream by one of the suppliants, saying :— ' So that peace and order may be restored to the Empire I will make a worldly descent as a son of Tokimasa'. In the light of this divine revelation Yoshitoki, the son, and Yasutoki, the grandson of Tokimasa, may be regarded as incarnations of the God Hachiman " (*N. B. Z. h.*, Vol. XXI, p. 16).

On one hand, in Israel, the invading armies of Babylonia and Assyria conquered the Israelites and took them in slavery to the banks of the Euphrates. There the national catastrophe that had come upon their people was interpreted by the prophets of Israel from their own higher ethical point of view, and, in consequence, some elements of universalism and individualism were introduced into the old national religion of Yahweh, thereby paving the way for the conversion, in the fulness of time, of the religious particularism or national religion of Israel into the world's religion of Jesus. On the other hand, in Japan, the formidable Mongol armada was bravely encountered and repulsed by the tremendous efforts of the Japanese forces under the command of Hōjō-Tokimune strengthened by firm reliance on the Providential aid of the Japanese national deities, especially of Amaterasu-Ōmikami, the Ancestral Tutelary

Goddess of the Imperial family. Thus, signal victory, of which the Japanese navy may well be proud, was gained over the Mongols, and so was secured and maintained the nationality of Japan. The people have since entertained a feeling of national pride and strong faith that Japan, of all nations under the sun, is unique, rejoicing in the divine rule of one and the same Imperial dynasty, unbroken and co-eternal with Heaven and Earth.

Needless to add, such being the case, the people of Japan cannot help believing in the Providence of unseen help of the national deities on high ; and that, *ipso facto,* Shintō, as the national religion still living, will be alive forever, as long as the nation of Japan flourishes and ceases not to exist.

Yahwism, the national religion of Israel, gave way to the universal religion of Christianity, along with the cessation of the existence of the nation of Israel ; while Shintō, as the national religion of Japan, has continued, and will continue, because Japan as a nation has continued and will continue. Here we see the difference between the national religion of the Jews and that of the Japanese people, although each may be called a " chosen people ", and just therein exists one of the essential characteristics of Shintō.

The Emperor Gonara (1496–1557), invoking Amaterasu-Ōmikami, the Ancestral Sun-Goddess of Ise, prayed thus :—

> "Like unto the Sun's bright light, eternal,
> Shining from above the skies—
> Bless, Oh Goddess, with thy care supernal,
> Generations yet to rise!"

An utterance of the national religion of Shintō is heard again in the Imperial poem of the Emperor Meiji, who breathed his last in the year 1912 :—

" I pray that Thou wilt keep the people in peace forever
And guard my reign, Oh ! Thou Great Deity of Ise."[1]

---

1 I have taken the liberty of quoting my friend Dr. Holtom's translation of this renowned Imperial poem from his *Political Philosophy of Modern Shintō* (*T. A. S. J.*, Vol. XLIX, Part II, p. 231).

CHAPTER XX

Unique Position of Shintō Among the World's Religions

As we have seen above, Shintō—particularly State Shintō—through all the stages of its development from the beginning, is a national religion. Therefore, Shintō, as a national religion, never dies, it still is, and ever will be. The national religion of ancient Greece, that of early Rome, that of ancient Babylonia and Assyria, that of ancient Egypt, etc., all are no more. As Milton, in his famous ode, happily sings of the fate of national religions in the ancient lands :—

" Apollo from his shrine
　Can no more divine,
　　With hollow shriek the steep of Delphos leaving.
　　　　. . . . .

　In consecrated earth,
　And on the holy hearth,
　　The Lars and Lemures moan with midnight plaint;
　　　　. . . . .

　Peor, and Baalim,
　Forsake their temples dim,
　　　　. . . . .

And sullen Moloch fled,

....

Nor is Osiris seen

In Memphian grove, or green,

.... " (*Christ's Nativity*).

Shintō, on the contrary, has never passed away. Today it is, as it was yesterday, closely bound up with the Japanese nation, inseparably interwoven in the national life of one and the same Japanese people. It is no doubt true that Judaism and Brahmanism—Taoism may not be an exception—which are all national religions, still exist among their own respective peoples, but the Jews of today nowhere exist as a nation, while the Hindoos now are not the Hindoos of the age of Brahmanism before the rise of Buddhism, and Taoism is not the national religion of one and the same ruling House of China. We may say there is no other religion that, in the same sense of the term as Shintō, still exists as a national religion in close connection with one and the same nationality as well as the same ruling House from the beginning. This is owing to the permanence of the national life of the Japanese people, continually under the sovereignty of the same lineage.

Shintō, which is the national religion of Japan, goes hand in hand with the nation that gave birth to it. The nation believes itself co-eternal with Heaven and Earth, so the religion that cannot be severed from the nation as long as it exists will never fail. This peculiar feature of Shintō we call the *unbroken continuity of Shintō,* which is one of its unique characteristics. A short-sighted observer will probably say that a national religion is behind in development, compared with universal religions, that, to wit, the national religions of ancient Greece and Rome, as well as that of the Hebrews, are all superseded by the universal religion of Christianity, which is far higher in advancement than any of those national religions—in other words that the monotheism of Christianity went ahead, in development, of the heathen polytheism of the Greek and Roman religions, that the polytheistic national religions are lower in development than the monotheistic universal religion and that the same is the case with Shintō, the national religion of Japan.

In my opinion, however, this view contains a truth but not the whole truth. Shintō has a peculiar phase of its development incomparable with the national religions of ancient Greece or Rome or any other country of old. Although it is a polytheism through all the stages of its evolution, not without a tinge of monotheism or henotheism, it has greatly developed a phase of pantheism under the influence of Mahāyana Buddhism introduced from abroad, while it has evolved itself as an ethical religion, making the best use of both Confucian and Buddhistic ethical teachings. Thus developed, as we have seen in the preceding chapters, Shintō, though in its origin a nature religion, has, in its evolution, taken a spiritualistic and idealistic character and it has never failed to inculcate worship of its Deity *in spirit* and *in truth*. It has given us the fundamental ethical principle, " Sincerity " or " Truthfulness ", otherwise called " Uprightness ", just as Buddhism teaches " Unconditional Benevolence" and Christianity enjoins " Universal Love ". If account be taken of the " quality " instead of the " quantity " of Deity—I mean belief in a single god as against belief in many gods—in judging whether a religion is higher or not than other religions, we can conclude with good reasons that Shintō, though polytheistic from first to last, has become more and more spiritualistic and idealistic, as well as ethico-intellectualistic, in the long course of its development, and has evolved in its tenets an ethico-religious principle called Sincerity or Uprightness unsurpassed by the Christian ethico-religious principle of Love or the Unconditional Benevolence of Buddhism. This is the bright side or higher aspect of Shintō, never before pointed out, as I, an impartial student of comparative religion, have, for the sake of truth, endeavoured here to do. The Occidental student of Shintō has hitherto studied and introduced into his own land only its primitive phases, *i. e.*, the naturalistic or lower aspect of Shintō, being deterred from deeper progress by the difficulties in the way

of his mastering the numerous books or documents of
higher Shintō, full of the queer terminology of Confucian
ethics as well as the abstruse philosophical phraseology
of Buddhism, chiefly written in Chinese characters. It
need not be mentioned that these difficulties no doubt
present practically insurmountable barriers to the foreign
investigator of the religion.

Moreover, we are to recognize the truths of theanthropic faiths such as Buddhism, of the religions of
ancient Greece and Rome and of Shintō, with just the
same absence of prejudice as we do those of theocratic
religions such as Judaism, Islam and Christianity. Shintō, as a theanthropic religion, has culminated in Mikadoism or the Worship of the Mikado or Japanese Emperor, as a divinity, during his lifetime as well as after
his death, even in the ethical stage of its religious development, as the author of the *Nijū-Issha-no-Ki* has
already pointed out. Herein lies even at the present
day, in my opinion, the essence or life of Shintō, inseparably connected with the national ideals of the
Japanese people. Japanese patriotism, or loyalty, as you
might call it, really is not simple patriotism or mere
loyalty, as understood in the ordinary sense of the
word, *i. e.*, in the mere ethical sense of the term ; it is
more—it is the lofty self-denying enthusiastic sentiment
of the Japanese people towards their august Ruler, believed to be of something divine, rendering them capable

of offering up anything and everything, all dearest to them, willingly,, *i. e.*, of their own free will; of sacrificing not only their wealth or property, but their own life itself, for the sake of their divinely gracious Sovereign, as the example of the late revered General and Countess Nogi well illustrated; all this is nothing but the actual manifestation of the religious consciousness of the Japanese people.

This sentiment is truly characteristic of Shintō as a religion. You might, as Lafcadio Hearn happily does, describe it as the "religion of patriotism", although, as he frankly confesses, the unparalleled loftiness of the religious conception of fealty cherished by the Japanese people of a nationality unique is such that "so trite a word as patriotism is utterly powerless to represent it".

The late Prof. Royce of Harvard University, also emphasizes the religious aspect of the loyalty of the Japanese folk, when he says :—

"However far you go in loyalty, you will never regard your loyalty as a mere morality. It will also be in essence a religion. Loyalty is a source not only of moral but a religious insight. The spirit of true loyalty is of its very essence a complete synthesis of the moral and of the religious interests. The cause is a religious object. It points out to you the way of salvation" (Royce, *Sources of Religious Insight*, p. 206).

Thus, we see that the essence or life of Shintō is

even today expressed in the peculiar religious patriotism of the Japanese people glorifying their Emperor as the centre of faith. So we venture to define Shintō, whose vital essence has never been languished, but is, on the contrary, strongly and ceaselessly active in the heart and mind of the Japanese people, as follows :—

The vital essence of Shintō manifests itself in an expression of that unique spirit of the national service[1] of the Japanese people, which is not only mere morality but is their religion, culminating in Mikadoism or their own peculiar form of loyalty or patriotism towards the Emperor, who is at once political head and religious leader in a government constitutional yet theocratico-patriarchal.

Here we see that in Japan there still exists the singular fact of the unity of religious observance and political governance, or " Saisei-Itchi ", which has never been severed or discontinued.

As we have seen above, Shintō expresses its vital essence in Mikadoism or the Worship of the Japanese Emperor, so that the secularization of Shintō that has resulted is quite natural; by which we mean the view that Shintō is not a religion at all, but is, rather, a repertory of State ceremonials and national morality or

---

1 It is now customary to speak of "social service" in contrast with the older expression "church service". The special expression "national service," here used, is coined in keeping with this phraseology.

ethics, the former being conducted generally in Shintō shrines while the latter is inculcated in public schools through the canon of the Emperor Meiji's Edict on the Education of the young generation of Japan, promulgated in 1890, together with the same Emperor's Ordinance issued in 1882 to the soldiers and sailors of His Majesty's services. This is because in Shintō, or, more strictly speaking, in State Shintō, where the theanthropic expression of religion predominates as it does in the religions of ancient Greece and Rome, the object of worship is a secular ruler on earth in flesh and blood. In other words, it is because the Shintō religion is national, non-propagandistic, is of a nature of worldliness, so to speak, in contrast with Buddhism which—though likewise a theanthropic religion—is universal, individualistic, and propagandistic; while Shintō has a fair share of the nature of theanthropic religion with Buddhism, the latter, intrinsically monastic in its nature as well as in its origin, draws a strict distinction between monks and lay-believers. So understood, the modern secularization of Shintō is quite comprehensible and a matter of course.

And, besides, we must remember that both the Confucian scholars and the savants of Japanese classics of the Tokugawa Regime were as a rule anti-Buddhistic; the latter, somewhat chauvinistic, being averse to imported foreign teachings, and the former from the standpoint of Confucian moral philosophy which is widely different from the religion of the Buddha. The combined parties emphasized at will a secular non-religious signification of Shintō, which has naturally led to the present secular interpretation of Shintō generally.

After the Restoration of 1868, the Meiji Government finally proclaimed State Shintō as non-religious; and, in 1884, put it entirely apart from the Buddhistic and Christian religions and gave it a sphere of independent existence quite different from that of the foreign religions, thus furnishing State Shintō with an asylum in which, under the protective aegis of the political power of the secular Government, it is safe from interference by its two religious rivals.

Meanwhile we must not lose sight of a new religious aspect of Shintō, which specifically developed itself in the Tokugawa Regime. This new religious movement of Shintō we should like to call Sectarian Shintō in contradistinction to the State Shintō mentioned above. The characteristics of Sectarian Shintō as contrasted with State Shintō are as follows :—

Sectarian Shintō is now divided into 13 sects, mentioned by name in Book I of this treatise. Most of these had a personal founder, and some of them had their origin, as separate independent sects *de facto*, in the Tokugawa Regime. In each case where the sect has an individual personage as a founder, its religious faith or tenet has a tinge of religious individualism, through which every believer hopes to be saved, faithfully following the way indicated by the personal inner experience of such a personal founder. In this double sense, we may say that Sectarian Shintō is individualistic. At the same time, needless to remark, all the sects are ethical. In especial, the Kurozumi Sect, the Misogi Sect, the Konkō Sect, for example, are remarkably ethical in their teachings.

If Sectarian Shintō is individualistic and ethical, it is quite conceivable that it has a tinge of religious universalism, even though it is not quite relieved of the bond of national religion. Therefore it may be described as quasi-universal or semi-propagandistic in character, and thus Sectarian Shintō has in principle some approach to the genuine universal religions, Buddhism and Christianity. Most of the Shintō sects are national in one respect, because their religious observances are not a little connected with some of the national deities mentioned in the *Kojiki* and *Nihongi* myths, but in another respect some—at least one—of the Shintō sects have passed beyond the limits of national religion. To cite an example : the Konkō Sect which adores Tenchikane-no-Kami (a name never mentioned in the *Kojiki* or the *Nihongi*) or the Heaven-and-Earth-Including-Deity, *i, e.,* the Supreme Deity whose influences extend over the entire Heaven and the Earth, free of any racial

restriction or boundaries of nationality—in its worship
of this Deity the sect displays an aspect of Shintō as
a universal religion.

In order to emphasize this point, let us cite, as another instance, the Kurozumi Sect, whose founder, Kurozumi-Munetada, enthusiastically proclaimed Sincerity as
its fundamental ethico-religious principle.   With pro-
minence thus once for all given to this ethical tenet it
seems beyond dispute that therein exists a germ of religious universalism in Shintō.

It was the spiritual force of that ethical principle
—religious moralism—that gave to the prophetism of
ancient Israel a tinge of religious universalism which
ignores national barriers.   To the Israelite major prophets Yahweh is the hypostatized *Summum Bonum* or
moral Ideal for all nations.   As the religious history of
Israel shows us, the religious moralism of the prophets
led their religion, national in origin, to a universalism
and individualism in theory, fulfilled in praxis later on
in the Christianity of Paul, where " there is neither
Jew nor Greek, neither bondmen nor freemen, neither
male nor female, all being one in Christ Jesus."   Thus
in Christianity genuine religious universalism gained
ground.   Compared with the manner in which religious
universalism came into existence in Israel, the appearance of the Kurozumi Sect is very similar.   And so
Kurozumi-Munetada teaches :—

" The Kami who do guard this sacred soil —
The Buddha of the land where Hindoos toil —
Alike are they, in that they reign, in grace,
Where pure Sincerity fills every space."

Again, he says :—

" Fret not o'er cares of health or mind ;
To lose e'en life be thou resigned ;
Midst true Sincerity find rest,
In Earth and Heaven 'twill make thee blest !"

His religious moralism leads to universalism, when he says :—

" The noblest attribute possessed in life
Most surely is Sincerity of mind—
That shines serenely through the whole world's strife
And man to man in brotherhood doth bind."

Inoue-Masakane, the founder of the Misogi Sect, also says :—

"What is faith ? It literally means true heart, implying Sincerity in heart, which itself again is the essence of divine heart " (*Inoue-Masakane-Zaitōki*).

And thus, alike with State Shintō and with its Sectarian offshoots, the universal ethico-religious principle of Sincerity, otherwise termed Uprightness, spread its roots in the religious soil of Japan, just as the corresponding universal ethico-religious principle of Love, in Christianity, gained ground on the shore of Lake Galilee, and as Unconditional Benevolence, the concordant universal ethico-religious principle in Buddhism, flourished in the valley of the Ganges.

It may well be added here, by way of conclusion, that the tenets of Christianity, Buddhism, and Shintō, the three living religions of the world, bound by universal brotherhood in religious Japan, stand fundamentally on one and the same Truth or Principle. Vary though the religions do in form, yet in essence are they the same.

In this reconciling and harmonizing spirit a Japanese bard sings :—

> " By routes diverse men may the mountain climb,
> Each path presenting different views, sublime –
> But when to the proud summit they do rise,
> The self-same smiling moon doth greet all eyes."

FINIS

BIBLIOGRAPHY

BIBLIOGRAPHY

IN

ALPHABETICAL ORDER

The following list comprises the works to which reference is made in the present volume, although the author is well aware that he is none the less indebted to many other works not mentioned

A

Acts du IVe Congres International d'Histoire des Religions.

Ancient Japanese Rituals (English Translation by Sir E. Satow and K. A Florenz in *T. A. S. J.*).

Avesta.

Azumakagami or *Eastern Mirror* (History of the Kamakura Shogunate). 吾妻鏡

B

Ban-Nobutomo-Zenshū or *Ban-Nobutomo's Collected Works.* 伴信友全集

Banshin-Engiron or *Account of the Guardian Deities.* By Nissen. 日宜 雷神縁起論

Bilderatlas zur Religionsgeschichte (*Germanische Religion*). By D. Hans Haas.

Bōsō-Shiryō or *Historical Sources of Bōsō.* 房總史料

Bukkyō-Zensho or *Complete Collection of Buddhist Works.* 佛教全書

C

Children of the Sun. By W. J. Perry.

Chimyōbō-Gohenji or *Reply to Chimyōbō.* By Nichiren. 日蓮 智妙房御返事

Christ's Nativity. By Milton.

Chūchō-Jijitsu or *History of the Central Empire.* By Yamaga-Sokō. 山鹿素行 中朝事實

D

Daihatsu-Nehangyō or *Mahāparinirvāṇa-Sūtra* (Nanjiō's *Catalogue*, No. 118). 大般涅槃經

Daijingū-Sankeiki or *Diary of My Pilgrimage to the Ise Shrine.* By Saka-Shibutsu. 坂士佛 太神宮參詣記

Dainihon-Chimeijisho or *Topographical Dictionary of Japan.* By Yoshida-Tōgo. 吉田東伍 大日本地名辭書

Dainihonshi or *History of Great Japan.* By Tokugawa-Mitsukuni (and His Descendants). 德川光圀等 大日本史

E

Elementary Forms of the Religious Life. By E. Durkheim.

Engishiki or *Institutes of the Engi Period* (901-923). 延喜式

Engishiki-Shimmyōchō or *Registry of Shintō Shrines* (*Catalogue of the Names of Shintō Shrines*) *in the Engishiki.* 延喜式神名帳

Epistle to Hōjō-Tokimune. By Nichiren. 日蓮 與北條時宗書

F

Five Stages of Greek Religion. By Gilbert Murray.

Fūgashū or *Collection of Poems.* By Hanazono-Tennō. 花園天皇 風雅集

Fusōryakki or *Outline of the History of Japan.* By Kōen. 皇圓 扶桑略記

G

Gedō-Shōjō-Nehanron (Nanjiō's *Catalogue*, No. 1260). 外道小乘涅槃論

Gempei-Seisuiki or *Rise and Fall of the Minamoto and the Taira Clans.* 源平盛衰記

Gendō-Hōgen or *My Miscellaneous Writings.* By Bakin. 馬琴 玄同放言

Genkōshakusho or *Biographical History of Japanese Buddhism, Compiled in the Genkō Era* (1322). By Shiren. 師錬 元亨釋書

Gishi (*Wei Chih*) or *History of Gi* (Wei). By Chinju (Ch'ên Shou). 陳壽 魏志

Gochinza-Hongi or *Records of the Establishment of the Cuter Shrine of Ise.* 御鎭座本紀

Gorgias. By Platon.

Gunshin-Mondō or *Inquiry concerning the War-God.* By Ise-Teijō. 伊勢貞丈 軍神問答

Gunsho-Ruijū or *First Collection of Miscellaneous Standard Works.* By Hanawa-Hokiichi. 塙保己一 群書類從

Gyokuyōshū (Gyokuyō-Wakashū) or *Book of Jewel Leaves* (Collection of Japanese Poems). By Fujiwara-no-Tamekane. 藤原爲兼 玉葉集

H

Hachiman-Gudōkun or *Teaching of the War-God Hachiman in Plain Japanese for Beginners.* 八幡愚童訓

Handbook of Greek Religion. By Arthur Fairbanks.

Heike-Monogatari or *Narrative History of the Heike* (English Translation by A. L. Sadler in *T. A. S. J.*). 平家物語

Higher Aspects of Greek Religion. By Lewis R. Farnell.

Hishizume-no-Matsuri-no-Norito or *Ritual of the Festival of Appeasing the Fire-God.* 鎭火祭祝詞

History of Greek Religion. By Martin P. Nilsson.

History of Japanese Literature. By W. G. Aston.

History of Religion. By Allan Menzies.

History of Religions. By E. Washburn Hopkins.

History of Religions. By George Moore.

Hitachifudoki or *Ancient Topography of Hitachi Province.* 常陸風土記

Hokkekyō (Myōhōrengekyō) or *Saddharmapuṇḍarīka-Sūtra* (Nanjiō's Catalogue, No. 134). 法華經 (妙法蓮華經)

Hokke-Shintō-Hiketsu or *Esoteric Doctrine of Shintō, Seen in the Light of the Hokkekyō* or *Saddharmapuṇḍarīka-Sūtra.* By Nitchō. 日澄 法華神道祕訣

Honchō-Jinjakō or *Studies on the Japanese Shintō Shrines.* By Hayashi-Razan. 林羅山 本朝神社考

Honchō-Kōsōden or *Biographies of Venerable Buddhist Priests of Japan.*
By Shiban. 師蠻　本朝高僧傳

Honchō-Monzui or *Japanese Literary Gems.* By Fujiwara-no-Akihira. 藤
原明衡　本朝文粹

Honchō-Seiki or *History of Japan.* By Fujiwara-no-Michinori. 藤原通憲
本朝世紀

Honchō-Shosha-Ichiran or *List of Shintō Shrines.* By Sakauchi-Naoyori.
坂內直顯　本朝諸社一覽

Honzon-Mondōshō or *What Is to Be Worshipped?* By Nichiren. 日蓮
本尊問答抄

Hyakka-Zeirin or *Miscellaneous Works by Different Writers.* 百家說林

Hyōchū-Kofudoki or *Ancient Topographies Annotated.* By Kurita-Hiroshi.
栗田寬　標註古風土記

I

Ichijitsu-Shintō-Gen or *Essence of Genuine Unitary Shintō.* By Jitō. 慈
等　一實神道原

Iliad.

Imperial Japanese Poems of the Meiji Era. By F. A. Lombard.

Inoue-Masakane-Zaitōki or *Inoue-Masakane as an Exile in the Island of
Miyake.* 井上正鐵在島記

Ippen-Shōnin-Nempuryaku or *Abridged Chronological Biography of the
Buddhist Saint Ippen.* 一遍上人年譜略

Ise-Futamiya-Sakitake-no-Ben or *Difference between the Outer Shrine and
the Inner Shrine at Ise.* By Moto-ori-Norinaga. 本居宣長　伊勢二宮
さきたけの辨

Itōshi or *Topography of the District of Itō.* 伊東誌

Izumofudoki or *Ancient Topography of Izumo Province.* 出雲風土記

Izu-no-Chiwaki or *How to Make Clear the Meaning of the Divine Way.*
By Tachibana-no-Moribe. 橘守部　稜威道別

J

Jikkinshō or *Ten Discourses on Morality Illustrated by Historical Nar-*

rations. 十訓抄

Jingikun or *Shintō Teachings.* By Kaibara-Ekiken. 貝原益軒　神祗訓

Jingiryō or *Shintō Administrative Law.* 神祗令

Jingishōjū or *Notes on Shintō.* By Urabe-no-Kanena. 卜部兼名　神祗正宗

Jingi-Zensho or *Some Important Works on Shintō.* By Saeki-Ariyoshi. 佐伯有義　神祗全書

Jingū-Zōreishū or *Collection of Historical Fragments Relating to Both Shrines of Ise.* 神宮雑例集

Jinja-Inshin (a Buddhist Book on Shintō). 神社印信

Jinja-Keimō or *Introductory Study of Shintō Shrines for Beginners.* By Shirai-Sōin. 白井宗因　神社啓蒙

Jinja-Shikō or *My Personal View of Shintō Shrines.* By Ban-Nobutomo. 伴信友　神社私考

Jinnō-Shōtōki or *History of the True Succession of the Divine Emperors.* By Kitabatake-Chikafusa. 北畠親房　神皇正統記

Jōei-Shikimoku or *Administrative Code of the Jōei Era* (1232). 貞永式目

K

Kagurauta-Iriaya or *Commentary on the Divine Hymns.* By Tachibana-no-Moribe. 橘守部　神楽歌入綾

Kanekuni-Shintō-Hyakushu-Kashō or *Collection of a Hundred Poems on Shintō Composed by Kanekuni.* By Urabe-no-Kanekuni. 卜部兼邦　兼邦神道百首歌抄

Kankyō-Hachiman-Shō or *Impeachment of the God Hachiman.* By Nichiren. 日蓮　諌曉八幡抄

Kannon-Gyō or *Avalokiteśvara-Bodhisattva-Samantamukha-Parivarta of the Saddharmapuṇḍarīka* (Nanjiō's *Catalogue*, No. 137). 観音経

Katahisashi-Zempen and *Katahisashi-Kōhen* (Miscellaneous Works in Two Volumes by Saitō-Hikomaro). 齋藤彦麿　傍廂（前篇及後篇）

Kinkai-Wakashū or *Collection of Poems Composed by Minamoto-no-Sanetomo.* 源實朝　金槐和歌集

Kochō (of Gomizuno-Tennō) or *Butterfly.* (English Translation by A. L.

Sadler).　後水尾天皇　胡蝶

Kofudoki-Itsubun-Kōshō or *Fragments of Ancient Topographies with Explanatory and Critical Notes.*　By Kurita-Hiroshi.　栗田寛　古風土記逸文考證

Kogoshūi (of Imbe-no-Hironari) or *Gleanings from Ancient Stories* (English Translation by G. Katō and H. Hoshino).　齋部廣成　古語拾遺（英譯者加藤玄智及星野日子四郎）

Kojidan or *Old Stories.*　古事談

Kojiki (of Ō-no-Asomi-Yasumaro) or *Records of Ancient Matters.*　(English Translation by B. H. Chamberlain).　太朝臣安麻呂　古事記

Kojikiden or *Commentary on the Kojiki.*　By Moto-ori-Norinaga.　本居宣長　古事記傳

Kojiki-Hyōchū or *Records of Ancient Matters Annotated.*　By Shikida-Toshiharu.　敷田年治　古事記標註

Kokon-Chomonshū or *Famous Stories, Past and Present.*　By Tachibana-Narisue.　橘成季　古今著聞集

Kokushi-Taikei or *Collection of Some Important Works of Japanese History.*　國史大系

Kokusō-Hongi or *Chronicles of the Local Chieftains.*　國造本紀

Konjaku-Monogatari or *Miscellaneous Tales of Different Ages.*　By Minamoto-no-Takakuni.　源隆國　今昔物語

Koshiden or *Exposition of the Ancient Histories.*　By Hirata-Atsutane.　平田篤胤　古史傳

Kōtaijingū-Gishikichō or *Records of the Shintō Rites at the Inner Shrine of Ise.*　皇太神宮儀式帳

Kujiki (*Kuji-Hongi*) or *Chronicles of the Old Matters of Former Ages.*　舊事紀（舊事本紀）

L

Lehrbuch der Religionsgeschichte.　By P. D. Chantepie de la Saussaye.

M

Magical Origin of Kings.　By Sir J. Frazer.

Making of Religion. By A. Lang.

Manyōshū or *Collection of a Myriad Leaves* (Oldest Collection of Japanese Poems). 萬葉集

Masukagami or *Bright Mirror* (History of Japan). 増鏡

Michiae-Matsuri-no-Norito or *Ritual of the Festival of the Road Deities.* 道饗祭祝詞

Miryū-Shintō-Kuketsu(shō) or *Esoteric Knowledge of the Shintō Religion Attributed to the Emperor Saga.* 御流神道口訣（抄）

Miryū-Shintō-Shodaiji-Bushū or *Miscellaneous Discourses on the Shintō Religion Attributed to the Emperor Saga.* 御流神道諸大事部集

Mizukagami or *Water Mirror* (History of Japan). By Nakayama-Tadachika. 中山忠親 水鏡

Muṇḍaka Upaniṣad.

N

Nichiren-Shōnin-Goibun or *Posthumous Works of the Buddhist Saint Nichiren.* 日蓮上人御遺文

Nihon-Bungaku-Zensho or *Collection of Japanese Literary Works Published by the Hakubunkan.* 博文館 日本文學全書

Nihon-Daizōkyō or *Japanese Buddhist Trpiṭaka Collection.* 日本大藏經

Nihon-Gairaigo-Jiten. By K. Ueda and S. Kanazawa. 上田萬年金澤庄三郎共編 日本外來語辭典

Nihongi (*Nihonshoki* under the Superintendence of Toneri-Shinnō) or *Chronicles of Japan* (English Translation by W. G. Aston). 舍人親王等 日本紀（日本書紀）

Nihon-Isshi or *Supplement to the Nihonkōki or Later Chronicles of Japan.* By Kamo-Sukeyuki. 鴨祐之 日本逸史

Nihon-Montoku-Tennō-Jitsuroku or *Authentic Japanese History of the Montoku-Tennō Era.* 日本文德天皇實錄

Nihon-Reiiki or *Marvelous Tales Illustrated by the Buddhist Doctrine of Retribution.* By Keikai. 景戒 日本靈異記（日本國現報善惡靈異記）

Nihon-Sandai-Jitsuroku or *Authentic History of Japan in the Reigns of the Emperors Seiwa, Yōzei and Kōkō.* By Fujiwara-no-Tokihira (and

Others). 藤原時平等　日本三代實錄

Nihonshoki-Sanso or *Commentary on the Nihongi*. By Ichijō-Kaneyoshi. ·
一條兼良　日本書紀纂疏

Nihonshoki-Tsūshō or *General Commentary on the Nihongi*. By Tanikawa-
Kotosuga. 谷川士清　日本書紀通證

Nijū-Issha-no-Ki or *Notes on the Twenty-One Shrines*. 二十一社記

O

Odyssey.

Ōharai-no-Norito or *Ritual of the Great Purification* (English Translation
by K. A. Florenz in *T. A. S. J.*).

Old Testament.

Onchi-Sōsho or *Older Books Re-published*. 溫知叢書

Orientalische Religionen (*Kultur der Gegenwart*).

Oriental Religions in Roman Paganism; the Mysteries of Mithra. By
F. Cumont.

Origin and Growth of the Conception of God (*Hibbert Lectures*). By Count
Goblet D'Alviella.

Ōsumifudoki or *Ancient Topography of Ōsumi Province*. 大隅風土記

Ōtonohogai-no-Norito or *Ritual of Luck-Wishing of the Great Palace*
(English Translation by Sir E. Satow in *T. A. S. J.*). 大殿祭祝詞

Outline History of Greek Religion. By Lewis R. Farnell.

Owari-Meisho-Zue or *Illustrated Topography of Owari Province*. By
Okada-Bun-en. 岡田文園（啓）　尾張名所圖繪

Owari-no-Kuni-Atsuta-Daijingū-Engi (*Kambyō-Engi*) or *Sacred History of
the Deity of Atsuta*. 尾張國熱田太神宮緣起（寬平緣起）

P

Political Philosophy of Modern Shintō (*T. A. S. J.*). By D. C. Holtom.

Primitive Mentality (English Translation by Lilian A. Clare). By Lucien
Lévy-Bruhl.

Psychology of the Religious Life. By George M. Stratton.

R

Rāmāyana (English Translation by M. N. Dutt).

Rāmāyana (English Translation by R. T. H. Griffith).

Reikiki or *Spiritual Essence of Heaven and Earth.* 麗氣記

Religion of Ancient Egypt (Hibbert Lectures). By P. le Page Renouf.

Religion of the Primitives. By Alexander le Roy.

Religions of Eastern Asia. By Horace G. Underwood.

Religions of the World. By E. O. Barton.

Religious Thought of the Greeks. By Clifford H. Moore.

Ressei-Zenshū or *Collected Works of the Japanese Emperors of All Ages.* By C. Furuya. 古谷知新　列聖全集

Rg Veda.

Rokudai-Shōjiki or *Records of Historical Events during the Reigns from the Emperor Takakura to the Emperor Gohorikawa.* 六代勝事記

Ruiju-Fusenshō (Sajōshō) or *Collection of Government Orders, Classified.* 類聚符宣抄（左丞抄）

Ruiju-Jingihongen or *Fundamental Studies of Shintō, Classified.* By Watarai-Ieyuki. 度會家行　類聚神祇本源

Ruiju-Kokushi or *Japanese History Classified.* By Sugawara-no-Michizane (and Others). 菅原道眞等　類聚國史

Ruiju-Sandai-Kyaku or *Government Orders in the Reigns of the Emperors Saga, Seiwa, and Daigo, Classified.* 類聚三代格

Ryōbu-Shintō-Kuketsushō or *Esoteric Knowledge of the School of Dual Shintō.* By Minamoto-no-Yoshiyasu. 源慶安　兩部神道口訣抄

Ryō-no-Gige or *Commentary on the Taihō Code under the Auspices of the Government.* By Kiyohara-no-Natsuno (and Others). 清原夏野等　令義解

Ryō-no-Shūge or *Collection of Various Commentaries on the Taihō Code.* By Koremune-no-Naomoto. 惟宗直本　令集解

Ryūkyū-Kokujiryaku or *Outline of the History of the Loo-Choo Islands.* By Arai-Hakuseki. 新井白石（君美）　琉球國事略

S

Saishi-Zatsui or *Miscellaneous Collection of Shintō Cults.* By Amano-Nobukage. 天野信景　祭祀雑纂

Saiten-Kaifushō or *Purport of Dual Shintō.* By Sōji. 僧慈　祭典開覆抄

Sangokuiji or *Gleanings from Histories of the Three Countries.* By Ichi-nen. 一然　三國遺事

Schintoismus im Japanischen Nō-Drama (Mitteilungen der Gesellschaft für Natur- und Völkerkunde Ostasiens, Bd. XIX). By Wilhelm Gundert.

Seibokukō or *Notes on Genuine Divination.* By Ban-Nobutomo. 伴信友 正卜考

Sengohyakuban-no-Uta-Awase or *3,000 Stanzas Submitted to the Ex-Emperor Gotoba in Imperial Poetry Competition.* 千五百番歌合

Senjishō or *Learn Buddhism in Time.* By Nichiren. 日蓮　撰時抄

Settsufudoki or *Ancient Topography of Settsu Province.* 攝津風土記

Shaku-Nihongi or *Commentary on the Nihongi.* By Urabe-no-Kanekata. 卜部懐賢　釋日本紀

Shasekishū or *Gleanings in Shintō and Buddhist Fields.* By Mujū-Hosshi (Mujū-Hōshi). 無住法師　沙石集

Shimanekenshi or *History of Shimane Prefecture.* By S. Nozu. 野津左馬之助　島根縣史

Shimmyōchō or *Registry of Shintō Shrines (Catalogue of the Names of Shintō Shrines).* 神名帳

Shimmyōchō-Kōshō-Dodaifukō or *Supplement to Ban-Nobutomo's Commentary on the Catalogue of the Names of Shintō Shrines.* By Kurokawa-Harumura. 黒川春村　神名帳考證土代附考

Shin-Butsu-Myō-ō-ron or *Transcendental Harmony between the Shintō Deities and the Buddhas.* By Nittatsu. 日達　神佛冥應論

Shindai-Kuketsu or *Esoteric Knowledge of the Divine Age.* By Imbe-no-Masamichi. 忌部正通　神代口訣

Shinka-Jōdan or *Tales Told by Shintō Priests.* By Mano-Tokinawa. 眞野時繩　神家常談

Shinkishū or *Collection of the Emperors' Autographical Writings.* By C. Furuya. 古谷知新　宸記集

Shinsen-Kisōki or *New Book on Divination.* 新撰龜相記

Shinsen-Shōjiroku or *Catalogue of Family Names Newly Compiled by Prince Manta (and Others).* 萬多親王等　新撰姓氏錄

Shinsen-Shōjiroku-Kōshō or *Commentary on the Catalogue of Family Names Newly Compiled by Prince Manta.* By Kurita-Hiroshi. 栗田寬　新撰姓氏錄考證

Shinshūi-Wakashū or *New Collection of Poems.* By Fujiwara-no-Tameaki 藤原爲明　新拾遺和歌集

Shintō (Hibbert Journal, Vol. XIX, No. 3). By Thomas Baty.

Shintō-Ame-no-Nuboko-no-Ki or *Heavenly Jewel Spear Record.* By Izawa-Nagahide. 非澤長秀　神道天瓊矛記

Shintō-Denju or *Shintō Doctrine Esoterically Preserved.* By Hayashi-Razan. 林羅山　神道傳授

Shintō-Dōitsu-Gemmishō or *Harmony and Unity of Shintō and Buddhism.* By Nikkō. 日珖　神道同一鹹味抄

Shintō-Gobusho or *Shintō Pentateuch.* 神道五部書

Shintō-Myōmoku-Ruijushō or *Things Shintoistic, Classified and Explained.* 神道名目類聚抄

Shintō-Shihon-Engi or *Historical Origin of the Four Discourses on Shintō.* By Tachibana-no-Sanki. 橘三喜　神道四品緣起

Shintō-Shoden-Kuju or *Introduction to Shintō Orally Given.* By Tomobe-no-Yasutaka. 伴部安崇　神道初傳口授

Shintō-Sōsetsu or *Collection of Miscellaneous Treatises on Shintō.* By N. Yamamoto. 山本信哉　神道叢説

Shintō-Sōsho or *Collection of Miscellaneous Works on Shintō.* By H. Nakajima and H. Ōmiya. 中島博光及大宮兵馬　神道叢書

Shintō, the Way of the Gods. By W. G. Aston.

Shintō-Uden-Futsujoshō or *Purport of Purity Revealed by the Divine Crow.* By Kamo-Norikiyo. 賀茂規清　神道烏傳拂除抄

Shin-Zoku-Kokin-Wakashū or *New Collection of Poems, Ancient and Modern,*

Continued. By Kasugai-Masayo. 飛鳥井雅世　新續古今和歌集

Shoki-Shūge or *Commentary on the Nihongi.* By Kawamura-Hidene. 河村秀根　書紀集解

Shoku-Nihongi or *Chronicles of Japan Continued.* By Sugano-Mamichi (and Others). 菅野眞道等　續日本紀

Shoku-Nihonkōki or Nihonkōki (Later Chronicles of Japan) Continued. 續日本後紀

Shosaishin-Ryakki or *Brief Account of Different Shintō Deities.* By Koike-Izumo. 小池嚴藻　諸祭神略記

Shōtoku-Taishi-Denryaku or *Biography of the Crown Prince Shōtoku* (by an anonymous author of the Heishi). 平氏　聖德太子傳曆

Shugendō-Shōso or *Works on the Shugendō or Buddhism Amalgamated with Shintō.* 修驗道章疏

Shuju-Onfurumai-Gosho or *Nichiren's Epistle to the Buddhist Nun Kō-nichi.* By Nichiren. 日蓮　種々御振舞御書（與光日尼書）

Sōsōryō or *Administrative Law of the Funeral of the Dead.* 喪葬令

Sources of Religious Insight. By J. Royce.

Study of the Development of Religious Ideas among the Japanese People as Illustrated by Japanese Phallicism (T. A. S. J.). By G. Katō.

T

Taiheiki or *Narrative History of the Reign of Peace.* 太平記

Takahashi-Ujibumi or *Traditional Narrations Preserved by the Takahashi Family.* 高橋氏文

Tamadasuki or *How to Worship the Shintō Deities.* By Hirata-Atsutane. 平田篤胤　玉襷

Tamuramaro-Denki or *Life of Sakanoue-no-Tamuramaro.* By Saga-Tennō. 嵯峨天皇　田邑麻呂傳記

Tennō-Hongi or *Chronicles of the Emperors.* 天皇本紀

Tōdaiji-Yōroku or *Annals of the Buddhist Temple Tōdaiji.* 東大寺要錄

Tōgoku-Ryokōdan or *Travels in the Eastern Provinces.* By Jukakusai. 壽鶴齊　東國旅行談

Tosa-Nikki or *Diary of My Journey Homeward from the Province of Tosa.* By Ki-no-Tsurayuki. 紀貫之 土佐日記

Tōshōgū-Goikun or *Moral Instructions Bequeathed by Tokugawa-Ieyasu.* 東照宮御遺訓

Toyouke-no-Miya-Gishikichō or *Book of Rites Relating to the Outer Shrine of Ise.* 豐受宮儀式帳

Transactions of the History of Religions.

U

Umpo-Irohashū or *Dictionary of the Japanese Language Alphabetically Arranged.* 運步色葉集

W

Wajin-Den (Wei Jen Chuan) or *History of the Japanese.* 倭人傳

Wakun-no-Shiori or *Dictionary of the Japanese Language.* By Tanikawa-Kotosuga. 谷川士清 和訓栞

Y

Yamatohime-no-Mikoto-Seiki or *Historical Records of Yamatohime.* 倭姫命世記

Yuiichi-Mondō-no-Sho-Kakitsugi or *Genuine Unitary Shintō with a Supplement.* By Inoue-Masakane. 井上正鐵 唯一問答書々繼

Yuiichi-Shintō-Myōhō-Yōshū or *Catechism of Genuine Unitary Shintō.* 唯一神道名法要集

Z

Zappōzōkyō or *Saṁyuktaratnapiṭaka-Sūtra* (Nanjiō's *Catalogue*, No. 1329). 雜寶藏經

Zasu-Nikki or *Imperial Buddhist Abbot's Diary.* By Gyōnyo. 堯恕 座主日記

Zeus, a Study in Ancient Religion. By Arthur B. Cook.

Zoku-Gunsho-Ruijū or *Second Collection of Miscellaneous Standard Works.* By Hanawa-Hokiichi. 塙保己一 續群書類從

Zokusajōshō or *Sajōshō (Collection of Government Orders Classified)* Con-

tinued. 欟左丞抄

Zoku-Shintō-Taii or *Outline of Popular Shintō.* By Hirata-Atsutane. 平
田篤胤　俗神道大意

Zoku-Zoku-Gunsho-Ruijū or *Third Collection of Miscellaneous Standard
Works.* By the Kokusho-Kankōkai (Japanese Books Publication
Society). 続々群書類從（國書刊行會）

──────────

INDEX

Kōkaku, 光格, 142.

Kokoro, 懐（心）, 34.

Kokūshin, 虚空神, 132.

Kokusō, 國造, 111.

Kokusō-Jinja (K. Shrine) of Aso, 阿蘇國造神社, 55-6.

Kokutai Shintō, 國體神道, 2.

Kōkyoku, 皇極, 103, 128.

Kōmei, 孝明, 29.

Komori-Machi, 子守町, 102.

Konda-Hachiman, 譽田八幡, 43, 51, 101. *Vide* Hachiman.

Kōnin, 光仁, 93.

Konkōkyō (Konkō Sect), 金光教, 1, 211.

Konoe, 近衞, 12.

Konohana-no-Sakuyahime, 木花開耶姫, 41, 72, 85, 116-7, 121, 131.

Kō-no-Miya, 國府宮, 154.

Konsei-Daimyōjin, 金勢大明神, 31.

Korea, 24, 28, 33, 34, 37, 48, 62, 70, 86, 89, 95, 111.

Koromonoko, 衣子, 124, 125.

Kōtoku, 孝德, 42, 105.

Kotoshironushi-no-Kami, 事代主神, 72.

Kowakubi, 強頸, 104.

Kōya, Mt., 高野山, 179.

Kṣitigarbha, 172.

Kuanyin, 觀音, 156,

Kuebiko, 久延毘古, 29.

Kugadachi, 盟神探湯, 41, 116.

Kuhao, 久波乎, 19, 60.

Kukunochi, 句々廻馳, 17.

Kumamoto, 熊本, 81.

Kumano, 熊野, 20, 61, 176, 180, 181.

Kumanukusubi-no-Mikoto, 熊野久須毘命, 71.

Kuni-no-Mihashira, 國御柱, 15.

Kuni-no-Sagiri-no-Kami, 國之狹霧

神, 132.

Kuni-Tokotachi (-no-Mikoto), 國常立（尊）, 65, 70, 131, 144, 186.

Kuraokami, 闇靇, 15.

Kurita-Hiroshi, 栗田寬, 18, 19, 60, 97.

Kurokawa-Harumura, 黑川春村, 78, 154.

Kurozumikyō (Kurozumi Sect), 黑住教, 1, 211, 212.

Kurozumi-Munetada, 黑住宗忠, 212.

Kusanagi-no-Tsurugi (Kusanagi Sword), 草薙劍, 21, 22, 23-4, 39, 94-5, 109, 114. *Vide* Divine Sword.

Kushimitama, 奇魂, 33, 34.

Kushinadahime, 奇稻田姫, 68, 73, 104.

Kusunoki-Masashige, 楠木正成, 160.

Kyōen = Keien.

Kyōto, 京都, 25, 75, 115, 188, 193, 198.

Kyūshū, 九州, 16, 28, 53, 89.

L

Lang, Andrew, 62, 64.

Laokoon, 176.

Laos, 33.

Lar, 202.

Lévy-Bruhl, Lucien, 79, 122.

Lemures, 202.

Lil, 33.

Livy, 85.

Lombard, F. A., 163

Loochoo, 琉球, 153.

Lowell, P., 52.

Lysandros, 50.

M

Maat, 71, 121.

Z

Zervanem Akaranem, 66, 132.
Zeus, 8, 14, 70, 71, 83, 123, 132, 133, 144, 148.
Zi, 33.

ERRATA AND CORRIGENDA

Page	Line	For	Read
39	18	48, 49	51, 52
198	29	-Suenari	-Narisue
247	6	-Suenari, 橘季成	-Narisue, 橘成季